Miami Herald

DWYANE WADE

HEART of the HEAT

30 YEARS

TRIUMPH BOOKS

T0164420

This book is available in quantity at special discounts for your group or organization.
For further information, contact:

Triumph Books LLC
814 North Franklin Street
Chicago, Illinois 60610
Phone: (312) 337-0747
www.triumphbooks.com

Printed in U.S.A.
ISBN: 978-1-62937-752-0

Miami Herald
Alex Mena / Sports editor
John Devine / Deputy Sports editor
David Santiago / Book Photo editor
Photographers: Jeffrey Boan, Al Diaz, Patrick Farrell, Hector Gabino, Carl Juste, Jared Lazarus, Walter Michot, Matias J. Ocner, Pedro Portal, Joe Rimkus Jr., David Santiago and Charles Trainor Jr.
Reporters: Israel Gutierrez, Dan Le Batard, Greg Cote, Michael Wallace, Joseph Goodman, Manny Navarro, Jordan McPherson, Barry Jackson, Anthony Chiang and David Wilson

Interior Design: Alex Lubertozzi
Cover Design: Jon Hahn

Front cover photo by Al Diaz / Miami Herald
Back cover photo by David Santiago / Miami Herald

PHOTOGRAPHERS
Miami Herald
Jared Lazarus: 1, 12, 15, 19, 24, 26, 30; Al Diaz: 2, 11, 16, 21, 33, 44, 59, 60, 62, 66, 72, 75, 79, 95, 107, 128;
Jeffrey Boan: 5, 9; Charles Trainor Jr.: 23, 43, 59, 69, 71, 81, 97; Hector Gabino: 29, 39; Joe Rimkus Jr.: 35, 37, 46, 98;
Patrick Farrell: 40; Carl Juste: 49, 51, 53, 54, 101; David Santiago: 65, 76, 82, 86, 88, 91, 103, 105, 109, 112, 119, 120, 126;
Pedro Portal: 93, 111; Walter Michot: 99; Matias J. Ocner: 100.

Additional Photos
AP Images: 7, 85, 115, 117; Getty Images: 56, 123, 124.

CONTENTS

Forwards Passed as Backcourt Gets Boost. 6

Heat Rookie, Fans Rise to Occasion in Victory 10

Dwyane Wade Pushes Fear, Mavericks Aside
with Season on the Line 14

Wade Has Heat a Win Away from Title with
Huge Effort. 18

Believe It: Miami Heat, World Champs 22

Dwyane Wade Helps Fulfill Title Promises
Made by Riley. 28

Wade on Olympic Team 34

Head of the Class. 38

MVP-Worthy 42

Wade County 48

Wade, LeBron on Same Team: Why Not? 52

The New Kingdom 58

Even Great Ones Need Help 64

LeBron James, Dwyane Wade Lead Way 70

Crowned 74

More Than Just a Flash of Greatness 80

Dwyane Wade's Unselfish Attitude 84

Healthy Dwyane Wade Working Wonders
for Miami Heat 90

Dethroned 94

Wade off the Court
and in the Community 98

Messy Breakup 102

Dwyane Wade's Return to Miami Filled with
Cheers, Emotional Moments 106

He's Back! 110

Back in It in a Flash 114

Dwyane Wade Reminds Us Why We'll Miss Him 118

One Last Team-Up. 122

Forwards Passed as Backcourt Gets Boost

By Israel Gutierrez • June 27, 2003

Last season, the Heat was fortunate enough to get an instant impact player when Caron Butler fell to the No. 10 spot. Thursday, the Heat showed attaining another impact player in the draft was still a high priority when it selected Dwyane Wade, a 6-4 guard from Marquette who is widely considered one of the most NBA-ready players in the draft.

While Heat coach Pat Riley said he expects Wade to contribute immediately, just how much might depend on what the team does with Eddie Jones.

Should Jones, constantly included in trade rumors, remain with the team, Wade would be expected to play the point guard and shooting guard positions. Should Jones be traded, the shooting-guard position would then be Wade's to handle.

Whatever Wade's responsibilities, Riley believes he is ready.

"He's a player," Riley said. "I'll tell you where he fits in. He, to me, is probably the most mature player that we worked out and scouted. Not only do I see him as a multiple-position player, but I see him as a guy who can defend.

"He's an absolutely complete player who's only going to get better, so we are absolutely excited with this pick."

Wade averaged 21.5 points, 4.4 assists and 2.2 steals last season, his junior year at Marquette. He played only two seasons of college basketball after sitting out his freshman year as a partial qualifier.

In his two seasons, however, Wade single-handedly resurrected the Marquette program. Last season, he led the Golden Eagles to the Final Four and was a first-team All-American.

Riley does not want to label Wade as a point guard or a shooting guard. Wade believes he is a combination guard who can handle either role. Wade said he spoke with Riley and that is what the coach said he expects of him.

"He just told me he wanted me to be a combo guard," Wade said. "He wanted me to play the [point guard] and the [shooting guard], and also that he wanted somebody to come in and play defense. Miami is known as a defensive team, and coming from Marquette, that's what Coach [Tom] Krean preached, so it's something I know I can come in and do."

Riley, who received consultation from Butler

Dwyane Wade shakes hands with NBA Commissioner David Stern after Wade was chosen by the Miami Heat with the fifth overall pick out of Marquette in the 2003 NBA Draft.

"He's one of the most mature young guys that I've ever met." —Pat Riley

on the Wade selection, said he was especially impressed with Wade's defensive ability.

"He's one of the most mature young guys that I've ever met," Riley said of Wade. "He's a complete player offensively, he has the skills to get to the basket, draw fouls and make plays. What I was most impressed by when I really studied him was his ability to defend people.

"I do believe this particular player, of all the players I've had in a long time, could probably play very comfortably in both spots. We're looking at a team possibly that has Wade, Jones, and Butler."

Riley said Wade had been high on the team's wish list since well before the draft. Toronto selected Georgia Tech freshman Chris Bosh with the No. 4 selection, leaving the Heat to select from a group that included Central Michigan center Chris Kaman, Kansas point guard Kirk Hinrich, and Texas point guard T.J. Ford.

Riley said had Bosh been available as well it would have forced the team to make a difficult decision. But the team is satisfied with the final result.

Jones, who watched the draft from his home in Weston, said he didn't anticipate the selection of Wade to affect his standing with the team.

"I think they took the best available player at the time," Jones said.

Jones was more concerned with what the team will do to continue to improve.

"I would like to see Alonzo [Mourning] sign back here," Jones said of his teammate, who will become a free agent July 1. "We've got a couple more dollars to spend on a free agent and hopefully we can get somebody."

As for Wade, Jones said he hasn't seen enough of him to assess his potential. Butler, though, said he played pickup games and AAU games against Wade and likes the idea of being on the same floor as Jones and Wade.

"To me it's like we're so long now," Butler said. "You're going to have Wade out there, myself, E.J., and Rasual [Butler]. We're going to be a force to be reckoned with.

"I think we all can take turns [handling the ball]. I could play point on a lot of possessions and Dwyane can switch up. We all can handle the ball, so it's just a matter of who wants it."

Wade, a husband and a father of a 16-month-old son, is also known for his ability to keep his teammates involved, which should also make him an instant favorite in Miami.

"I'm not going to change my game at all that way," said Wade, the Conference USA Defensive Player of the Year in 2003. "I love to see my teammates succeed. I think by giving your teammates confidence that you're going to give them the ball and you're not going to force a shot, they'll go to war for you also.

"I think if your teammates succeed, you succeed." ■

Wade shows off his brand new No. 3 Miami Heat jersey while coach Pat Riley holds Dwyane's 1-year-old son Zaire.

Heat Rookie, Fans Rise to Occasion in Victory

By Dan Le Batard · April 19, 2004

Forget the screaming disc jockey, the gyrating dancers and the famous songs piped in over the giant arena speakers to create a canned and familiar noise.

Miami Heat infant Dwyane Wade, a dazzling mixture of jazz and funk, was alone at the center of the stage now, being asked to perform.

Go ahead, kid.

The spotlight is all yours.

Make some music that moves us.

When Wade finally came down after his last-second, winning shot, AmericanAirlines Arena rose up, and the resultant 81–79 Heat victory over New Orleans in the first game of the NBA playoffs Sunday night had a smiling Wade dancing right at the center of this bobbing, screaming, clapping celebration he helped create.

It was a pretty cool thing to feel at your core.

South Florida, moved.

Wade had dragged 20,000-plus people of various origins, backgrounds, and beliefs out onto that dance floor with him.

And isn't that how it is with the best performers?

At the height of their excellence, they can bring us up there with them, where we all get to sway together.

You know what the rookie Wade did as punctuation after making his game-winning shot over New Orleans' two All-Star players?

He took his right fist and began pounding his heart.

After Miami had overcome a 10-point deficit and blown an 11-point lead, it was hardly the only one in this building taking a pounding.

It has literally been years since we've had basketball games that mattered like this one in South Florida, Miami having spent the past two seasons teetering between irrelevant and laughable. And playoff basketball is particularly rugged, Miami's undersized players spending as much time on the floor Sunday as in flight. It isn't ballet this time of year as much as it is wrestling.

You would think that combination of tension and trauma might leave a team as young as this one rattled, especially when playing a New Orleans Hornets team littered with so many veterans that it isn't so much a basketball squad as it is a basketball museum.

But at the end of Sunday's game, Heat coach

In Game 1 of the first round of the Eastern Conference playoffs, Dwyane Wade sank a two-pointer to give the Miami Heat an 81–79 victory over the New Orleans Hornets.

Stan Van Gundy placed the ball and the game in the impossibly large hands of his youngest player, who was also, it goes without saying, the youngest one on the floor.

The Hornets have things in their closet older than Wade. He was born in 1982. So here you go, kid. Hurry up and grow up, OK?

For a while there, with most Heat fans wearing giveaway black T-shirts, it felt like everyone was dressed appropriately for mourning. All that New Orleans experience had thundered back from a late double-digit deficit against a Miami team that appeared to be lost and tightening.

All that momentum Miami had built on a Wade dunk—the one after which he spread his arms wide, like a child playing airplane—had evaporated more quickly than a bad dieter's willpower.

The emotion and energy and vibrancy of youth? New Orleans looked like it was going to be able to withstand the Heat.

But then the ball was placed in Wade's hands at the top of the key, time ticking down, just Wade and New Orleans' best player isolated with every eye in the building on them.

Wade did not shrink from his moment.

He rose to meet it.

And allowed everyone in the building to take flight with him. ■

In Wade's rookie season, he led the Heat to the Eastern Conference semifinals for the first time since 1999–2000. In the postseason, he averaged 18 points, 5.6 assists, and four rebounds per game.

Dwyane Wade Pushes Fear, Mavericks Aside with Season on the Line

Wade Was Afraid But Never Doubted He Could Save Heat's Season

By Dan Le Batard · June 15, 2006

Were you afraid, Dwyane?

Miami Heat guard Dwyane Wade lets the question sit there for a second and stares at you in silence.

Did you ask something stupid? Have you insulted him? Trying to recover, you stammer something about the season collapsing all around him. You replace the word "fear" with the word "doubt." He interrupts quickly this time, saying, "Not doubt. Never doubt. Never, ever doubt."

But then he stops.

Stops and goes back to your original question.

Goes back to being afraid.

"Yeah, you fear," Wade said of Tuesday's deficit against the Dallas Mavericks in the NBA Finals. "I was afraid. There's something wrong with you if you aren't afraid. The building was quiet. Our season was slipping. I was afraid."

The Mavericks' Dirk Nowitzki was nervous in a Game 1 with few consequences, and he had one of his worst games of the playoffs. His teammates, Jason Terry especially, bailed him out. Wade was nervous in Game 3 with a season's worth of consequences, and all he does is save the season.

Down 13 points in a fourth quarter the Heat needed more than any it has ever played, the hero was straight-up scared. Isn't that what the philosophers say is the definition of courage? Not the absence of fear but the ability to overcome it?

Wade only overcame it with the single best playoff game a member of the Miami Heat has ever played. This is not open for discussion. No one has ever been bigger in a big moment for the Heat than Wade was in saving the Heat's season Tuesday.

It wasn't just his 42 points. It wasn't just his 13 rebounds. It wasn't just the 15 points he scored in a desperate fourth quarter on a bad knee and with lingering flu and five fouls.

In 2005–2006, Dwyane Wade led the Miami Heat to its first NBA Finals. For the season, he averaged 27.2 points, 6.7 assists, and 5.7 rebounds per game and made his second straight All-Star Game.

It was every little thing he did. One turnover? One?! And how about what you don't see on the stat sheet. For example, Wade soared in to grab the rebound on Nowitzki's free-throw miss with three seconds left as Shaquille O'Neal sat and James Posey had trouble keeping Jerry Stackhouse away from a crushing tap-in. That rebound was Stackhouse's for the taking. He began the free-throw attempt behind Posey but ahead of Wade and moved Posey under the rim, into bad position. But Wade soared in and took the game from him.

"I'm pretty sore," he says after midnight Tuesday.

In Game 3 of the 2006 NBA Finals, with the Heat down 2–0 in the best-of-7 series, Wade powered the Heat to a 98–96 victory, leading both teams by scoring 42 points and bringing down 13 rebounds.

Wade has just finished postgame interviews at the podium, and he gets up with a grimace and a groan. It is how someone 60 years older than him might rise from a table. The grimace and groan will return a few minutes later, when he tries to drop himself gingerly into the back of a cart that will escort him back to the locker room. That's what he left on that court in saving Miami's season. Rising up to meet and surpass some of the world's greatest athletes at the height of sports has left him so spent that he needs a ride back, so beat up that he would be unable to practice Wednesday.

"I wasn't able to explode because of my knee," Wade says. "I could barely dunk."

There is a flammable rivalry in Wade's draft Class of 2003. Heat coach Pat Riley challenged Wade by looking around the locker room before a playoff game against the Detroit Pistons and telling Wade to make others witness him become the first crowned champion. Never mind that second pick Darko Milicic won one on the bench in Detroit. The use of "witness" was purposeful. It is the word around which the commercial campaign of No. 1 pick LeBron James of Cleveland revolves. Make LeBron witness, Dwyane.

Dallas Maverick Josh Howard is an exceptional, underrated player from that class, and he would like to elevate himself into the James-Wade discussion. Howard scored 21 points Tuesday, and Dallas had been 25–0 when he did that. But Howard scored zero in the fourth quarter while Wade was scoring 15. Howard, 2003 or no 2003, is not in Wade's class.

"You know what is weird?" Wade asks, limping between the podium and the cart. "My most confident point in the entire game was when we were down 13 points."

Huh?

You were scared but confident in the fourth quarter?

How can that be?

"Because I said to myself that I wasn't going out like this," he says. "I'm going out shooting. I'm going out fighting. I'm not going out like this. I'm going to soar. I've done it before in fourth quarters. We've done it before in fourth quarters. I was going to get the crowd back into it and feed off the energy. I'm telling you, I was most confident when we came out of that timeout."

Quite the flight, from sore to soar.

There's still a mountain to climb, of course. Dallas is begging Antoine Walker to shoot, and he is obliging much too much. Udonis Haslem, whose desire is overwhelming and inspirational, is being left open because he is wounded. And Dallas is up 2–1 in the series even though Nowitzki is capable of having the kind of game Wade just did but hasn't yet. Still, Miami has a mighty little weapon that fears but does not doubt.

Is this the highest emotional moment you've had in basketball, Dwyane?

Wade lets the question sit there for a second again, then laughs.

"Nah," he says. "My highest emotional moment hasn't happened yet."

Another laugh.

"Not yet. ∎

Wade Has Heat a Win Away from Title with Huge Effort

By Israel Gutierrez · June 20, 2006

One of Michael Jordan's most memorable moments, his game-winner over Bryon Russell in Game 6 of the 1998 NBA Finals, is widely considered an offensive foul that went uncalled.

So the fact that Dwyane Wade's heroic effort in Game 5 of these NBA Finals was blended with controversial foul calls, noncalls and timeout calls probably won't stain the accomplishment that has placed the Heat one win away from its first NBA championship.

"He's the best right now, and that's all you can say," Shaquille O'Neal said of his teammate. "He's the best."

Wade's 43 points were a career best in the postseason, but Wade himself likely would not call this his best playoff performance ever. That's because it began as one of his worst. The Dallas defense was determined to pay more attention to Wade whenever the dynamic shooting guard even came close to approaching the basket.

Wade started out 3 of 14 from the floor, and when he looked like he might begin to get it going, the Mavericks attempted to intimidate him with hard fouls, the most obvious coming at the 4:34 mark of the third period when Erick Dampier sent him to the floor and Josh Howard stood over him momentarily. Wade told the Mavericks players, "That don't work," as he approached the foul line, but it still would be a few more minutes before he proved it.

"Their defense was, I think, geared to him," Heat coach Pat Riley said. "He was 3 for 13 in the first half. He was having a hard time finding spaces and gaps."

The only constant for Wade throughout the game was his ability to get to the free-throw line. Even before he piled up 21 points in the fourth quarter and overtime, the 6-4 guard already had taken 16 free-throw attempts, setting the tone for what would be his finest moment.

"You know, when you make free throws, it puts you into a rhythm," Wade said. "Early on, I missed some shots I normally hit. But give them credit, they did a good job of making me take tough shots. I kept going, kept attacking.

"Second half, I came out and tried to get to the hole more, and like I said, the whole thing was, they were trying to not let me get there. You saw the segment, it was four hard fouls in a row. It got

Dwyane Wade reverse dunks during the 2006 NBA Finals. He led all scorers once again in Game 5 versus the Dallas Mavericks with a career playoff-high 43 points.

me into a flow and got me kind of mad at the same time. I was ready, I told Shaq, 'I'm with you, man.'"

Said Riley: "He's very, very smart when they are in the penalty. They got in the penalty third quarter, fourth quarter, a little bit early, and when they are in the penalty, he's not going to accept anything else but go to the basket.

"So he gets fouled a lot on the floor and guys are bumping and banging on him, and he gets to the line. So it's one of the benefits of actually having Shaquille when they started to hack him, they got into the penalty rather quickly in overtime, and he gets to the line."

It was Wade's final trip to the line, however, that will be questioned until these Finals are completed. Before Wade ever got a chance to score on the final possession with the Heat trailing by a point, the Mavericks contend that Wade committed a backcourt violation.

James Posey inbounded the ball to Wade, and replays showed that Wade simultaneously caught the ball while leaping with one foot into the backcourt. Wade was allowed to catch the ball in the backcourt, but had the officials determined Wade's left foot was still in the frontcourt when he made his initial contact with the ball, it would have been called a backcourt violation and given the Mavericks possession.

With no call being made there, Wade turned to his right and found a double-team of Devin Harris and Jason Terry. Before Wade was able to split that double-team, he could have been called for an offensive foul against Terry, who fell to the sideline after some contact with the driving Wade.

With no call there, Wade continued to the basket, this time finding Harris, Adrian Griffin, and Dirk Nowitzki in the way. Wade drove between Harris and Nowitzki to attempt a scoop shot. The official watching the play from behind, Bennett Salvatore, called the foul on Nowitzki for putting a hand on Wade's lower back as he was in the air attempting the shot.

The Mavericks believe that wasn't a foul, but photos showed Harris fouling Wade across the right wrist as he attempted the shot, which could have explained why Wade missed the layup attempt so hard off the backboard.

Wade insisted after the game that he was fouled, saying he got hit twice on his way to the rim. But the player known for his poise in the clutch still had to make two free throws.

He made the first, then had to sit through a timeout that the Mavericks didn't even want called at the time, and came back to make the second.

"There was no question in my mind I was going to make them," Wade said. "There was no question in any of my teammates' minds I was going to step up there and make them."

That put an end to arguably Wade's most memorable playoff game. But all it means is that the Heat must win a game in Dallas, which is the site of two of Wade's most uneven games in this postseason.

In the Heat's first two games of the Finals, Wade averaged 25.5 points but shot just 17 of 44 (38.6 percent) from the floor with nine total turnovers.

"When you go on the road and you don't play good games, then you turn the ball over, it's hard to win," Wade said. "But we took our two losses and

After being down two games to none in the 2006 NBA Finals, Wade led the Heat to three straight victories over the Mavs, putting them up 3–2 in the best-of-7 series and one win from the franchise's first NBA championship.

came back home and got better and won a dramatic game in Game 3, and our confidence got really, really rolling after that. We've been playing on a high level. We have to continue to do it. We're up 3–2, and for us to win everything, we have to go out there and win one in Dallas.

"It's going to be very tough, but that's why we play this game, for these moments, so [I'm] looking forward to it."

And if matters get tough in Dallas, everyone knows who the Heat will turn to, no matter how he has performed to that point.

"I have a lot of faith in him," O'Neal said. "We all have faith in him. We just give him the ball and he does what he does. He's a very unselfish player, a very great player. It's not too many times that he starts off slow and he stays slow.

"Dwyane is just a fabulous player." ◼

Believe It: Miami Heat, World Champs

By Greg Cote · June 21, 2006

DALLAS—Smiling and hugging and screaming and dancing and blowing kisses and raising index fingers and pounding on their hearts and high-fiving and laughing and raising their arms in triumph, the best basketball team South Florida has ever seen held up the golden trophy at midnight here Tuesday night.

Mountain, climbed.

Basketball, conquered.

History, recorded.

Miami 95, Dallas 92.

The champion Miami Heat.

Hold on a second.

Let that one marinate for a second.

The champion Miami Heat.

Let's start that again.

Just to let it soak in so you know you weren't dreaming last night.

The champion, champion, champion Miami Heat is the best basketball team in the world, and it is a startling, flabbergasting, wonderful thing to say today—and forevermore. Let history record that it wasn't but four games ago that this season looked spent, down 13 points with six minutes remaining in the fourth quarter and down 2–0 in this series.

But the Mavericks exhaled to enjoy the view before completing the climb. And an avalanche by the name of Dwyane Wade fell on their stunned heads as, mouths agape, their season was suddenly buried in sand.

Get used to this, South Florida.

Wade isn't done.

No, he's just getting started.

"I can't wait to get back to Miami, man," he said afterward through a smile that wouldn't leave his face.

And, again, Wade is just getting started.

Finishing? It wouldn't be surprising if Alonzo Mourning, Gary Payton, and even Pat Riley decided to retire with this as the view. Riley is greedy about greatness, but he was made weary by this climb and needs hip replacement surgery, and he has finally delivered on the promised parade down Biscayne Boulevard that he talked about upon arriving in 1995.

"That stupid comment," he has called that promise in the decade since.

But now it is reality, all Tuesday's joy about to spill into Miami's streets in coming days until

Miami Heat guard Dwyane Wade dishes the ball off while being guarded by Dallas Mavericks forward Dirk Nowitzki during the 2006 NBA Finals.

the parade—a parade that had been mapped and planned by Dallas, routes and times, when the Mavericks were up 2–0. Oops.

"Very motivating," Wade called that. "We wanted it. And we took it."

Mourning was exceptional Tuesday, setting picks, blockings shots, flexing muscles. He was the face of the franchise once, the face of frustration and almost and pain. Playing on a borrowed kidney, he wanted in an uncommon way Tuesday. He blocked five Mavericks shots in 14 minutes. And you should have seen the smile spread across his face as he held up that trophy.

"My doctor told me I could have a drink," he said afterward, drenched in champagne. "I hadn't had a drink since my diagnosis in 2000. My doctor will give a doctor's note for today."

Once Miami took the lead, it never trailed again.

Wade was booed during introductions. Booed louder than he was in his first two games here. Booed louder than Shaquille O'Neal, even. That's the sound of respect. As Reggie Jackson once said, they don't boo nobodies.

Dallas jumped to a 26–12 lead, but Finals MVP Wade wasn't having that. And from that point on, you could feel the life leaking out of the building.

Surely, the Mavericks could, too. What began as a mushroom cloud of noise, angry and loud, soon became silent fear—so silent that you could hear Mourning's echoing screams reverberate after he dunked with hostility upon the head of poor DJ Mbenga. Another Mavs miss? The arena groaned in unison. Another Wade make? The arena sagged

Miami Heat players and coaches celebrate the team's first ever NBA title after taking Game 6 against the Mavs 95–92, to win the series 4–2.

in unison. The precious home-court advantage? It evaporated right before your ears.

Dallas led by 14 in the first quarter. Miami sliced it to nothing. Dallas led by 10 in the second quarter. Miami took away the lead with another angry burst. The Dallas crowd and Dallas players seemed to have this in common—terror. They were feeding each other negativity like an abusive and dysfunctional relationship. Dirk Nowitzki scored the last basket of the half for his 17th point, an exceptional total, but this was met with only a smattering of muffled applause. Miami led 49–48.

Dallas' nice, little, second-place season was down to a half.

And Miami had the most dangerous assassin on the court.

David Stern might as well have handed Miami the trophy right then.

The life leaked out of this Dallas building, this Dallas team, this Dallas season. In all my years covering sports, I've never once been in a building that felt this afraid for game-related reasons. For an injury to a star player slumped on the ground, yes. For a team falling flat, no. If not for the music thumping, the electric and sexy Dallas dance team would have been gyrating in complete silence in the third quarter. Oh, wait. What's that little racket? Oh, never mind. It was the sound of a small pocket of traveling Miami fans clacking a clacker imported from South Florida.

So the ball got heavier, as if it were filled with 40 pounds of sand. The rim got smaller. Throats constricted. Wade had put the fear of Michael Jordan in them. And breathing became difficult until, finally, Dallas expired.

Nowitzki scored 29 points, only two of them in the fourth quarter. Jason Terry scored 16 points, none of them in the fourth quarter. Wade, meanwhile, was smiling and laughing and passing the ball behind his back as the Mavs let subs Marquis Daniels and Jerry Stackhouse take all the important shots.

The Mavs appeared allergic to the rim. They settled for jumper after clanking jumper. And it's hard to make those when your hands are shaking. Dallas shot a brutal 37 percent and was beaten by a Miami team that missed 16 of its 18 three-pointers. Up six with 3:41 left, Miami could hear the "Let's go, Heat!" chant from its tiny pocket of fans. Up five with 17.7 seconds left, Dallas fans evacuated as if the building was on fire, that "Let's go, Heat!" chant chasing them to the exits. A curious choice of music came next—"It's Getting Hot in Here."

Heat hot.

"Let's hear a big round of applause for your Dallas Mavericks," the PA announcer implored as Miami danced and hugged and screamed and held up the trophy.

But you didn't hear much of anything from the stunned crowd.

All you could hear, above it all, above the entire sport, was the celebrating Miami Heat.

The champion Miami Heat. ■

Wade clutches the NBA championship trophy after the Heat's Game 6 victory in Dallas. Named the 2006 NBA Finals Most Valuable Player, Wade led all scorers with 34.7 points per game, while also averaging 7.8 rebounds and 3.8 assists.

Dwyane Wade Helps Fulfill Title Promises Made by Riley

By Israel Gutierrez • June 25, 2006

It wasn't Dwyane Wade who said he envisioned a parade down Biscayne Boulevard back in 1995, when he was hired to bring a championship to Miami.

That was Pat Riley's pseudo pledge.

It wasn't Wade who stood in front of AmericanAirlines Arena upon his arrival in 2004, when he promised the considerable gathering of fans that he would bring a title to Miami.

That was Shaquille O'Neal's guarantee.

Yet there was Wade, scoring 15 points in the fourth quarter and bringing his team back from 13 down to help deliver on those promises.

There was Wade, scoring 43 points, his best playoff game ever—including the last two nerve-wracking free throws with 1.9 seconds on the clock—to help deliver on those promises.

There was Wade, scoring 36 more in the final game of the season, including four more huge free throws, to help deliver on those promises.

And there was Wade, accepting the NBA Finals MVP trophy in the center of the American Airlines Center floor, after he delivered on those promises.

It wasn't Wade who was supposed to be the main reason the Heat is a championship franchise. Not in 1995, and not in 2004.

But now that Wade has done it, the 6-4 guard in just his third year in the NBA has catapulted himself from a rising superstar to a still-dribbling legend. His 34.7-point scoring average in the Finals was more than even Michael Jordan in his first trip to the championship round—and those comparisons were being tossed around even before Wade completed his magical run to a title.

And now it's Wade that has people believing that the promise of another championship is very much a possibility.

"He just took it to another level," Riley said of Wade. "You all witnessed it. You all watched it. Players like that are very hard to come by, and to watch them grow right in front of you, you know, he's making his legacy in his third year. So, I mean, we are so blessed to have him."

Wade already had been considered one of the

Dwyane Wade shows off the Larry O'Brien NBA championship trophy to about 250,000 joyous Miami Heat fans during the team's victory celebration in downtown Miami on June 23, 2006.

best players in the league entering the Finals, but just where he stood in that debate was always in question. So having been given the biggest stage in basketball, Wade made his case.

Games 1 and 2 in Dallas were hardly strong arguments in Wade's favor. Coming off a flu that limited him in Game 6 of the Eastern Conference finals, Wade was still a bit weak and somewhat bothered by the new slew of defenders the Mavericks were throwing his way.

"He wasn't tentative," O'Neal said of Wade's opening games of the NBA Finals. "He was just trying to keep people involved. You know, it's our job to make him look good, and, you know, a lot of people didn't play well in Game 2, including myself."

Through 42 minutes of Game 3 in Miami, as the Mavericks were taking a 13-point lead and looking to grab a commanding 3–0 lead on the Heat, Wade had been less than spectacular again.

With his season on the line, though, Wade exploded for 12 points in the final 6:15 to bring his team back from the depths of despair. And so began his legendary Finals rebirth.

Wade followed up his 42-point Game 3 with 36 more in a 24-point blowout in Game 4. Then, in case anyone still questioned Wade's ability to come through in the clutch, he scored 21 points in the fourth quarter and overtime of Game 5, including the game-tying basket in regulation and the game-winning free throws with 1.9 seconds remaining in overtime.

All that was left to complete the masterpiece was a breakthrough road performance in Game 6.

Miami Heat coach Pat Riley talks to Wade during a break in a game during the 2005–2006 season.

Wade was as smooth in Dallas as he had been the previous nine quarters in Miami, hitting shots from any and every spot on the floor, demoralizing the Mavericks, who twice saw double-figure leads disappear behind the will of Wade.

Even players like O'Neal, Antoine Walker, and Gary Payton—veterans who once held their previous franchise's fates in their hands—were willing to let Wade hold their fortunes in his massive mitts.

"Wouldn't you?" Riley said. "All of those guys experienced the same thing for years and years, the ball kept coming to them, coming to them, coming to them, coming to them.

"No, I don't think they ever deferred to him. They have so much respect for him because they trusted him. They trusted that he wasn't for himself only. They trusted that he was all about winning and that, you know, a team of veterans can turn over something to him that's valuable to them because they know he's going to deliver. So Dwyane is probably one of the most respected young players this game has had in a long time. I think he proved a lot in the last four games, this sweep, the last four games."

Since that four-game stretch, Wade's name has been mentioned with some of the greatest, including Jordan, whom Wade grew up watching in his hometown of Chicago.

And while he'll fight off those comparisons at every opportunity, he is thankful he now has one more trait in common with Jordan.

"I remember when the Bulls won their first championship, sitting at home on my floor watching the games," Wade said. "And then Jordan did his famous shot [against the Lakers], I went right in the backyard, turned the lights on and couldn't do it myself. I had no athletic ability. I was young.

"I've been a big dreamer all my life, and I'm going to continue to be a big dreamer. The Bulls were a special team, and I'm just happy that I can sit up here and talk about them now."

Now others are talking about Wade as the best the NBA has to offer.

"When you have the title, until someone takes his belt, I'd have to say yes," ESPN analyst Greg Anthony said on espn.com when asked if Wade is the best player in the league. "Remember, he was beyond great. No one, and I mean no one, could be any better than D-Wade was in the Finals. He is the best, period."

Even Riley, who watched a magician at his very best, said Wade is incomparable.

"You knew Magic [Johnson] was always going to make the right play, get the ball to the right person, be able to absolutely dictate the tempo of the game, and also make big plays," Riley said.

"But, no, I've never had a player like this—or I have not been around a player who can absolutely, at times, beat five guys, and then at the same time, make great plays to players."

He makes promises that much easier to fulfill.

"I made that promise because of D-Wade," O'Neal said. "I knew he was a special player.

"I know that being on a championship-caliber team, you've got to have a great one-two punch—and D-Wade is a fabulous player."

"To me, it's still crazy when I walk around and I see people wearing my jersey, people wearing my shoes, the demand for 'Wade' stuff," Wade said. ∎

Wade goes in for a flying tomahawk dunk during the 2006 NBA Finals.

Wade on Olympic Team

By Michael Wallace · June 24, 2008

Miami Heat guard Dwyane Wade had a message for skeptics who believe he's taking a big risk by pushing his recovering left knee through a summer of Olympic play: Get used to it. And get over it.

"I can't see how I'm taking a risk," Wade said Monday during a teleconference. "No one has given me any real reason how I'm taking a risk [by] playing basketball at the highest level. I really have no comment for that other side who say that. They're irrelevant to me."

Wade, one of 12 players officially named Monday to the national team roster for the Beijing Summer Olympics, insists he is many things as he prepares for the USA's training camp this weekend in Las Vegas.

Healthy. Hungry. Excited. Focused. Angry. Yes, even angry. Wade said he is driven by redemption in his quest to help Team USA recapture a gold medal in international play for the first time since the 2000 Games.

Joining Wade on the national team Olympic roster are guards Kobe Bryant, Jason Kidd, Deron Williams, Chris Paul and Michael Redd; forwards LeBron James, Carmelo Anthony, Tayshaun Prince, and Carlos Boozer; and centers Dwight Howard and Chris Bosh.

The roster was announced Monday in Chicago, where Wade has been training for nearly six weeks to convince USA Basketball managing director Jerry Colangelo and team coach Mike Krzyzewski that he has recovered from knee problems that ended his Heat season in March.

The Heat had been publicly supportive of Wade's wishes to participate in a hectic Olympic schedule. But team officials also have said Wade is making a personal decision to commit to a training camp on July 20 that follows with nearly a month of travel and exhibitions leading to the August 10 Olympic opener against China.

Colangelo said he has read reports and heard speculation about some teams having reservations about their players committing to the Olympics. Those concerns, in part, led to Colangelo reaching out in recent days to Heat president Pat Riley regarding Wade's potential status.

"I had a conversation with Pat Riley—one final time, just to talk about their interest in having [Wade] participate," Colangelo said Monday. "Did they have any reservations? [They were] totally supportive, want him to play, think it's all part of his rehab. And to be quite honest, think this is going to help prepare him for the next season for the Miami Heat."

Colangelo also had attended one of Wade's training sessions, and the two spoke at length about

Dwyane Wade made his second U.S. Olympic basketball team in 2008, after playing for the 2004 team that won a bronze medal in Athens, Greece.

"I'm healthy [and] I haven't felt this way in two years. I'm excited. But I'm angry and focused again." —Dwyane Wade

his progress. But Krzyzewski said Monday that he would seek clearance from the Heat's medical staff before Wade participates in July's training camp.

The plan is then to determine how to proceed in games. With Kidd, Bryant, James, Anthony, and Howard set as starters, Wade is expected to come off the bench in a role similar to the one he played in 2006 during the World Championships in Japan.

"It's not like I'm playing 48 minutes a night," Wade said. "It's not like I'm doing a [whole] season."

Wade, a four-time All-Star and 2006 Finals Most Valuable Player, said he is motivated to return with a gold medal after he finished with a bronze medal in his previous two missions. He also played on the 2004 Olympic team that finished third in Athens.

On Monday, Colangelo and Krzyzewski sounded as if Wade's spot on the current team, which included a potential pool of 33 players, was never seriously in doubt if he proved to be willing and relatively healthy.

Krzyzewski said that courtesy was established back in 2006, when Wade followed through with his national team commitment just weeks after leading the Heat to a championship.

"He had just had an amazing year—one of the special years in the history of our game," Krzyzewski said. "He was beat up, too. He wasn't at 100 percent. A lot of guys would have begged out of it [national team play]. Some guys would have said they were hurt a little bit more than [they were]. [But] he showed up. That's why he's so valuable. Just watching his smile today made me feel good."

"I'm healthy [and] I haven't felt this way in two years," Wade said. "I'm excited. But I'm angry and focused again." ■

Along with teammate Kobe Bryant (left), Wade helped USA Basketball return to international dominance, winning gold in the 2008 Summer Olympics in Beijing, China.

Head of the Class

Wade's Play in '08 Prompts MVP Talk

By Israel Gutierrez · December 11, 2008

You couldn't help but lightly scoff at those overzealous Heat fans who were chanting "M-V-P" for Dwyane Wade before even a quarter of the season was completed.

Sure he's leading the league in scoring and all, but shouldn't you worry about staying in a playoff hunt before you start demanding postseason hardware?

Then Wade dunked on Emeka Okafor's head and finished with 41 points in a tight win and it suddenly became more than a little bit OK. In fact, it would be a disservice not to at least discuss the possibility of Wade earning the league's top individual honor, because frankly, we've never seen anything like this down here in 21 years of NBA existence, and the league has barely seen anything like it in its entire history.

Up until this year (and excluding that two-week period in June 2006), Wade has always been the underdog in any discussion regarding the best player in the league. Perhaps it was because his long-range jump shot wasn't consistent enough, or because his defense left something to be desired, or because that 320-pound parasite attached to him was sopping up all the credit the past few years.

There was always a reason to rank Wade slightly behind Kobe Bryant or LeBron James based on some minor deficiency.

That can't happen anymore. At least it shouldn't. Because Wade has not only rounded off his game to become arguably the most complete player in the league, he's also simply outperforming the others normally placed in his category.

For those who thought his efficiency with more shot attempts and no Shaquille O'Neal would suffer, Wade is shooting a career-best clip while leading the league in shot attempts.

For those who assumed his assists would drop and turnovers rise with supposedly lesser talent surrounding him, he's dishing at a career pace while cutting his turnover averages from the past two seasons.

For those who thought Wade would never be a defensive presence, he has become arguably the most disruptive perimeter presence in the league, collecting timely steals, influencing other turnovers and blocking shots at a pace no other guard can close match.

MVP talk might as well start now, because it's only going to continue.

The difference between Wade this year and

Dwyane Wade had arguably his best regular season statistically in 2008–2009, when he averaged 30.2 points, 7.5 assists, and five rebounds per game, and also made his fifth straight All-Star team.

"What he's doing in terms of steals and blocks, I don't know how many 6-4 NBA players have ever been able to do that before in this game."

—Erik Spoelstra

Wade of 2006 comes down to two areas: an extended shooting range and a commitment to defense.

His comfortable shooting range has stretched to about 20 feet. Yes, he's hitting a handful of threes, but it's the long two-pointer that is suddenly so consistent it makes defending him officially impossible.

"If I shoot 15 in a game, I feel like I should hit 13," Wade said. "That's how comfortable I am with it."

Defensively, Wade isn't foolish enough to believe he can shut down scorers by himself. Nobody actually can (no, not even Ron Artest or Bruce Bowen or Bryant). He's instead combining that explosive athleticism with his great floor vision (yes, there's such a thing on defense) to make running offense chaotic for the opposition.

"I think he should be a First Team All-Defensive guy this year," Heat coach Erik Spoelstra said. "What he's doing in terms of steals and blocks, I don't know how many 6-4 NBA players have ever been able to do that before in this game."

What's left to scrutinize? Even those who claim Cleveland's King would be putting up better numbers if he were actually playing in fourth quarters need only look at the statistics per 48 minutes to see Wade is still sitting on top (he only averages two more minutes a game than LeBron).

There's really only one factor that would keep some from joining in the Wade for MVP talk: about 40 more wins.

If there has been one constant in NBA MVP voting, it's that the winner always comes from a team sitting at or near the top of the standings. Wade won't win it with a surprising 45-win campaign and a No. 5 playoff seed. James averaged 31 points, seven rebounds, and six assists for a 50-win Cavs team in 2006 and still was a distant second to Steve Nash.

"Kobe has had years where he just murdered the league, but his team was .500 and he didn't get MVP," Wade said.

It will take a complete assassination of the league and a top-four playoff seed for Wade to garner true consideration. Without it, Spoelstra's more likely to win Coach of the Year than Wade picking up a trophy.

But there are no such criteria for chanting M-V-P. Although with 31 home games left, you might just want to pick your spots. ∎

Wade drives to the basket against Cleveland Cavaliers forward LeBron James during a regular-season game in 2008–2009.

MVP-Worthy

Dwyane Wade's Star Keeps Burning Brighter

By Greg Cote · March 11, 2009

An athlete has gained admittance to that rare place just beyond superstardom when the highlight-reel nights are expected, and the excellence assumed. When stupefying becomes the norm. And so when that running three-point shot of his kissed through the net as the buzzer blared and the home arena turned to bedlam Monday night, that really wasn't so extraordinary at all.

That was just Dwyane Wade.

Nobody on the globe is playing better basketball right now.

No athlete for any South Florida team has been better at what he does.

Dan Marino came closest—can it really have been a quarter century ago?—yet heroics in football are different. He required plenty of help on the receiving end of his passes to set all those records in 1984.

Wade does it seemingly by himself, winning games and making the Heat matter again through his hell-bent will and sheer skill.

Chicago's John Salmons ought to have filed a police report for the way Wade picked him clean of the ball in the closing seconds of the second overtime Monday, then arched home a clock-beating three-point shot for a 130–127 victory.

"He came out of nowhere," Salmons would depose later.

It was a dramatic finish even by Wade standards, causing him to leap onto the scorer's table and thrust his arms high as the merry din engulfed him.

"Always wanted to do that," he'd say afterward, grinning.

The snapshot was of a player in his physical prime at age 27 and on top not only of that scorer's table but of his game and his sport.

None other than good buddy LeBron James text-messaged congratulations.

The game-winner gave Wade 48 points for the night along with 12 assists and four steals. Ho hum.

Was it really that much better than his 42 points against Toronto a few nights earlier? Or the 41 he scored against the Cavaliers? Or the 46 that led the miracle rally past the Knicks? Or the 50 he dropped on Orlando?

Or whatever he might have planned for the visiting Celtics on Wednesday evening?

How do you quantify electrifying?

What athlete, in any sport, is more on top of his game than Wade is right now?

All at once his nickname, Flash, seems an

Dwyane Wade steals the ball from the Bulls' John Salmons in the final seconds of a tied, double-overtime game at home on March 9, 2009, before draining a game-winning, three-point basket at the buzzer.

understatement. Wade cuts to the basket quick as a beam leaves a flashlight. It's a wonder his sneakers can keep up.

"Like a bat out of hell," in Kobe Bryant's words.

There is a word for the kind of NBA season Wade is having and especially for the tear he has been on the past month or so:

Jordanesque.

Said teammate Jamario Moon after the latest installment of Wade's World: "Right now, man, there ain't nobody in the league playing better."

Heat coach Erik Spoelstra, in his postgame comments, put it plain.

"Mr. Dwyane Tyrone Wade Jr.," he began, "if he is not legitimately considered for an MVP candidate, I don't know what [else] he has to do."

Wade's friend and text-message buddy, Cleveland's King James, is commonly considered the league MVP front-runner with the Lakers' Bryant his nearest competition in what generally has been seen as a two-man race.

That needs to change. Right now.

James and Bryant are worthy candidates both by their own individual statistics and (as much) by the fact their teams have the two best records in the league.

The thing is, Wade has better overall numbers individually, and without question is relied upon more by his team and therefore more valuable *to* his team.

Wade comfortably leads the NBA with a 29.7 scoring average, is second in steals, is top 10 in assists and is on pace to block more shots than anybody his height in history. (Did I mention his

Wade goes in for the slam dunk during a game in the Heat's first-round playoff series against the Atlanta Hawks in 2009.

"Mr. Dwyane Tyrone Wade Jr., if he is not legitimately considered for an MVP candidate, I don't know what [else] he has to do."

—Erik Spoelstra

five three-pointers Monday were a career high?)

The Cavaliers and Lakers are so good they probably still would be playoff teams this season without James and Bryant. But the Heat without a healthy Wade likely would be headed closer to last season's embarrassing 15–67 record than to the playoffs.

Miami is only 1½ games off pace from earning home-court advantage in the playoffs just one season later, and the difference, quite simply, is a healthy Wade. A fully recovered, intensely motivated, better-than-he-ever-was No. 3.

He elevates the game of the young players around him—Michael Beasley, Mario Chalmers, Daequan Cook—every bit as palpably as he elevates in the paint toward another slam dunk.

He is the NBA's leading scorer and absolutely indispensable to and the cause of the league's most improved team. That sounds like an MVP.

Wade's profile was similarly high in the summer of 2006 when he led the Heat to its NBA championship and was Finals MVP. But Miami's fall to last year's shambles was mirrored by Wade's

own tumble due largely to shoulder and knee injuries.

"I can't believe how quickly we don't matter," Wade said last season.

Just as quickly, the Heat matters again on account of one player's rebound to elite status.

Wade's season seems all the more superhuman for the very human issues he has confronted off the court. An acrimonious divorce has included charges of infidelity and a custody fight over his two young children. An eponymous restaurant chain failed. A disgruntled former business partner made public allegations of pot smoking by Wade.

Only on the court has the young man found refuge and been in control.

Wade has the option to become a free agent and elicit offers from other teams in the summer of 2010, but the Heat should have no priority greater than to re-sign him. This season has made that plain, with Monday night the exclamation.

"This is my house!" he'd screamed into the din from atop that scorer's table.

May it remain so for years and years. ∎

Wade puts up a fadeaway jumper against the Orlando Magic during a 2008–2009 regular-season game in Miami.

Wade County

Guard's Playoff Career-High 46 Keep Miami Alive

By Michael Wallace · April 26, 2010

Eventually, Heat players insisted, if they kept kicking, there would be a breakthrough after so many losses. Eventually arrived Sunday.

With Dwyane Wade doing the bulk of the swinging, the Heat booted this series back to Boston for Game 5.

Wade scored a playoff career-high 46 points, including 19 in the fourth quarter, to help Miami stave off elimination with a 101–92 victory Sunday at AmericanAirlines Arena.

Where there was a will for the Heat, there was, thankfully, a Wade.

Two days after dehydration and cramps knocked him out of the final stages of a 100–98 loss in Game 3, Wade delivered the devastating blows down the stretch to knock out Boston and allow his team to maintain a postseason pulse.

"He's that type of player," Heat forward Quentin Richardson said of Wade's latest heroics. "Sometimes, he comes out and puts a cape on."

Down 3–1 in the series, the Heat still faces overwhelming odds in its quest to become the first team in NBA history to overcome a 3–0 deficit. But Miami isn't looking that far down the line just yet. The focus is solely on getting a win Tuesday in Boston and bringing the series back to Miami for a Game 6 on Thursday.

Still, Sunday's victory was a major breakthrough for the Heat, which had lost 14 of its past 15 games against Boston. That stretch included six consecutive losses this season and four in which Miami led in the fourth quarter before stumbling to defeat.

But even after squandering an 18-point first-half lead Sunday and trailing by seven in the third quarter, Wade refused to let the Heat fall. The start of the offseason will have to wait at least a few more days.

"I just ain't ready for the summer yet," said Wade, who will be one of the most sought-after free agents in league history July 1. "It was time to be aggressive. Very aggressive. I was going to shoot those shots no matter what happened. I got hot at the right time. Once I get into a rhythm, I think I can make any shot."

Wade didn't miss many. He was 16 of 24 from the field, including 5 of 7 from three-point range. In the process, Wade set franchise playoff records for points, points in a half (30), and made shots (16).

But he also got plenty of help. Richardson had 20 points, Michael Beasley had 15 and Udonis

Dwyane Wade elevates for a jump shot over Boston Celtics guard Ray Allen. Wade scored a career playoff-high 46 points against the Celtics in Game 4 of the Miami Heat's first-round playoff series against the Celtics.

"Clearly, after this game he's moved into first place as the best player to come out of Marquette." —Doc Rivers

Haslem led the Heat with 11 rebounds.

Wade scored 11 points in a row starting late in the third quarter, a barrage that sparked a 25–7 run to put Miami ahead 93–82 with 6:13 left in the fourth.

At that point, it was Boston's turn to falter amid a late-game stretch of uncharacteristic mistakes. The Celtics were outscored 30–15 in the fourth, when they shot 29 percent and missed eight of 11 free throws.

Boston missed five consecutive foul shots after it pulled to within 96–92 with 2:36 left. That stretch included three consecutive misses from Ray Allen, one of the most accurate free-throw shooters in NBA history, and two misses by Kevin Garnett.

Rajon Rondo had 23 points to lead Boston, which also got 18 points and 12 rebounds from Garnett, 16 points from Pierce and 15 from Allen.

"It's very uncharacteristic for us," Garnett said of the late-game meltdown. "We had our chances.

For some reason, the things we usually do very well that got us to 3–0 in the series, we were terrible at that."

But Wade was brilliant in bringing back memories of the 2006 NBA Finals, when he pushed Miami back from a 2–0 deficit to win the series with a string of 40-point games.

"It's another chapter," Wade said, comparing Sunday's effort to his vintage playoff performances in 2006. "Just the energy—what the playoffs bring out of you. Whenever you feel your back's against the wall, something happens."

Wade is shooting 60.5 percent and averaging 33.8 points, six assists, and five rebounds in the series. He has been a royal headache for Celtics coach Doc Rivers, who, like Wade, starred in college at Marquette.

"Clearly, after this game he's moved into first place as the best player to come out of Marquette," Rivers said. ■

Wade drives past a screen set by Heat point guard Mario Chalmers against the Celtics.

Wade, LeBron on Same Team: Why Not?

By Dan Le Batard · June 27, 2010

Dwyane Wade and LeBron James are always talking about what great friends they are. They are so bonded by shared sensibilities and experiences and excellences that Wade would stay at James' mansion when the Heat played in Cleveland. Both men say winning matters most. And here they are, at a career crossroads together, and all they have to do to find the best teammate available to them in free agency is look at each other.

Three years ago, they talked and decided together to sign similar contracts so that now, in a few days, they would have the same freedom of choice at the same time. In other words, they planned this; they've already teamed to make one really big business decision at a time of maximum value. Everything that has happened in the time since—Wade exiting national relevance early every postseason while required to do too much heavy lifting alone, James winning every individual accolade without winning anything that matters—brings them together now with just the right amount of appreciation and frustration and freedom and power and perspective in their prime.

Why in the name of all that is holy and sane wouldn't they choose each other?

Isn't this simple?

Hog the championships. Own the sport they love as young men. Make millions upon millions of dollars while teaming on commercials and winning and having fun. We can quibble about if their games fit together, which means you'd be arguing that it is better to have Amare Stoudemire with Wade than LeBron Bleeping James, but otherwise the only thing keeping them apart is something we all learn as little kids.

Sharing.

That's Plan A for salesman-to-the-stars Pat Riley, who has pushed all his chips to the middle of the table on free agency with a suited ace and a King. Riley knows how star-struck and event-driven this market can be. He copyrighted basketball flash and glitz in Los Angeles. He knows James-Wade will sell here in a way that Joe Johnson won't. So his job and his legacy now is to convince these two to share the stage and glory and fame the way he once sold Kareem Abdul-Jabbar, basketball's all-time leading scorer, on the hypnotic powers of Magic.

The entire upbringing and wiring of Wade and James in sports has preached team, harmony,

Selected in the same NBA Draft Class of 2003, Dwyane Wade (picked fifth) had made six straight All-Star teams by 2010, while the Cleveland Cavaliers' LeBron James (picked first) had also made six straight All-Star teams and had just collected his second consecutive league MVP award.

unity, and the importance of sacrifice, but here's the problem: maybe neither of them wants to be Scottie Pippen. Athletes tend to lie or lack self-awareness when they say that all they want to do is win. What they really want is to be the reason for said winning. Michael Irvin articulated that well when he got bummed watching teammate Alvin Harper running toward the end zone in the Super Bowl with his football.

Maybe this is childish or maybe it is human nature, but there's something about this arena that turns muscular men into infants. That isn't a criticism. Growing up is overrated, and being a kid is forever fun. But you know that goofy thing the Cavs did before games? Where all the other players would gather for a team photo and James would kneel down and pretend to snap their picture with an imaginary camera?

You have to convince James to share that play camera with Wade and hope they don't fight over it. That's all you have to do for James and Wade to get all the toys and turn the league into their personal playpen.

It seems pretty simple, doesn't it?

Share winning with your friend or play defense to keep him from it? What would you do if it was your good friend?

Winning and championships are going to take a back seat to something as silly as Wade feeling threatened by a bigger star coming to his city? A-Rod was LeBron in this scenario once. He didn't come and steal New York from Derek Jeter.

Last week, I put the question to two basketball Hall of Famers, one NBA coach and one NBA

Wade and James, who had become friends off the court, embrace on the court during the 2009–2010 season.

owner: why wouldn't two great players and great friends do this?

The owner said, "Ask Orlando and Tracy McGrady and Grant Hill how that works. One friend may like a great sports town. The other may like the beach. And friends don't mean there are two balls in a game. LeBron and D-Wade both need the ball, and neither are knock-down shooters. So I don't know that those two together are better than LeBron with the cast he had in Cleveland. In fact, unless you got the right players, the Cleveland team is probably better."

The coach said, "Ego. Those two don't want to share the top billing. They want talent around them, but it has to be complementary talent. They want to win, but winning isn't the only thing or even the most important thing. The most important thing is their standing in comparison to their peers."

Charles Barkley said, "Attention. You'd be surprised how much guys want all the attention."

Only Isiah Thomas made it sound like it was any kind of possible. Thomas was a champion and Hall of Famer and star before he was the basketball coach at FIU. I asked him, in his prime, how he would have felt if someone of the stature of James came to his team to overshadow him.

"I would feel lucky," he said.

Not threatened?

"Sometimes the moment calls for you to step forward," he said. "Sometimes the moment calls for you to step back."

But what about the idea that stars don't merely want to win but want to be the reason for winning?

"Those are the guys who always lose," Thomas said. "Those are the guys that champions prey on. Those are the losers."

That sounds good, right? So do this:

"If real winning is what you are pursuing, ego and money and glory don't get in the way," Thomas said. "Great players always play well together until they win the championship. That's when the 'disease of more' creeps in. But LeBron hasn't won. There's always an ego sacrifice with winning. Pau Gasol and Ron Artest can do a lot more scoring elsewhere. Kareem was the greatest player ever, and he gave room to Magic. Do you want to be The Man or do you want to be a champion? What really matters to you?"

Thomas has been a coach for a long time now. He says the things coaches teach once they have wisdom and perspective.

He laments all the ego in this generation of players. Problem is, he also flashes a Hall of Famer's teeth when I asked him what he would do if he were LeBron.

"Show me the hardest challenge," he says. "I'd want to go to New York. That's the hardest place, right? Well, [bleep] you then. I'm going to do it there." ■

Wade and James during the medal ceremony at the 2008 Beijing Summer Olympics. The pair helped the U.S. basketball team to its first Olympic gold medal since 2000.

The New Kingdom

Rock Star Rally Greets New Trio for Miami Heat

By Israel Gutierrez · July 10, 2010

It was a celebration for three kings, in basketball shorts.

The rock star setting was so much for LeBron James, Chris Bosh and Dwyane Wade, the trio of NBA superstars now sharing the same stage in Miami, they couldn't contain themselves. They giggled, danced and whooped while waiting to be raised onto the AmericanAirlines Arena platform, literally rising from the floor in a cloud of smoke before 10,000 of their most devoted, delighted and delirious fans.

From the moment James, the NBA's two-time Most Valuable Player and arguably its most popular athlete, announced Thursday night on ESPN that he would be joining Wade and Bosh in Miami, the excitement has been off the charts.

So when Sam Bleeker, 23, heard there might be a formal coronation introducing the Heat's star-studded trio on Friday night, he and two friends drove down from Boca—just in case.

"They said it was going to be either Friday or Monday, so we came down," said Bleeker, a Heat season ticket-holder who stood in line by an employee entrance for three hours before the doors opened.

The Heat, working around the clock since James' announcement at 9:27 p.m. Thursday, sent out a release announcing the party details about 4 p.m. Friday. By 6 p.m., thousands had gathered outside the arena waiting to get a glimpse of the three together.

When the doors opened at 7 p.m., Dennis Correa, 25, of Kendall was among those who aborted all previous plans to be part of this historic moment in South Florida sports.

Correa said he watched James make his announcement from a Cheesecake Factory on a television with no sound, only captions.

"They had the sound down and I had to read it," said Correa, who heard of the event via Twitter and put down a deposit for season tickets just before his arrival. "When I saw the word 'South,' I went crazy. I kissed my dad on the head."

It was a full two hours between when the fans entered and when James, Bosh, and Wade made their entrance.

But no one seemed to mind. Fans carried posters featuring the three players in Heat uniforms and the slogan: "Yes. We. Did."

Others wore shirts celebrating the acquisitions, one of them reading "Let Them Hate," in reference

In the summer of 2010, Miami Heat general manager Pat Riley assembled the Big 3, adding two-time MVP forward LeBron James (left) and five-time All-Star center Chris Bosh (right) to the Heat's six-time All-Star guard Dwyane Wade (center).

The Miami Heat unveiled the Big 3 at AmericanAirlines Arena in Miami on July 9, 2010, for 10,000 excited fans.

to the backlash from Cleveland over James' departure.

"They got seven years with LeBron," said Nick Munez, 21. "They had their chance. It's time to win."

As they entered the main bowl and headed toward the backstage area, James, Wade, and Bosh couldn't hide from a group of lucky fans who saw them ushered through a crowd of media members and cameras.

They walked up steps onto the platform in full uniform, James wearing his new No. 6, Bosh in a new No. 1, and Wade in his familiar No. 3.

Chris Bosh, Dwyane Wade, and LeBron James acknowledge Heat fans from the stage set up at AmericanAirlines Arena during the rally on July 9, 2010.

"It's like the All-Star Game," Wade yelled over to James as they awaited instructions to step onto another platform that would elevate them to the top of the stage. Before that, they all paused to watch the big screen showing a collection of video montages of each player.

James placed his left leg on one of the rails as he watched, with a fitting tattoo that read HISTORY running down his leg.

Before they were introduced, Heat president Pat Riley, the architect of this unprecedented Heat trio, received a long ovation when the big screens showed him sitting in his usual seats along the south side of the building.

Then, finally, with smoke and pyrotechnics normally reserved for rock concerts, the trio was raised to the top of the stage. Bosh couldn't help but let out a scream that was swallowed by the deafening sound in the arena.

When they made it to the main section of the stage, Wade waved his hands and clapped, while James nodded and smiled, soaking in the results of his long-awaited decision.

"How do you like your Miami Heat now?" Heat television play-by-play announcer Eric Reid asked the crowd.

The trio walked down a catwalk, slapping hands with fans before settling into three stools, where they were awarded keys to the city and interviewed by Reid.

"It feels right," James said. "We're going to make the world know that the Heat is back."

James, Wade and Bosh, all of whom signed for less than the maximum possible contracts available to them for the sake of building a better team around them, followed that with a news conference.

At the end, each had a ceremonial signing of their contracts. The Sharpie markers used will be auctioned off, the details of which are yet to be determined, to benefit Heat charities.

It was the first of what's expected to be many parties now that James, Wade and Bosh have teamed in Heat uniforms with visions of winning not one, but several NBA championships in Miami.

"Even with just Wade and Bosh, we could build a team," said Jared Pittinger of Boca Raton. "Now with LeBron, everyone's gonna come to collect their rings down here."

Victoria Capuano, 26, of Brickell, said she plans to see every home game this year—her boyfriend has season tickets. Her favorite player was Michael Beasley, but if trading him will bring a championship, she said she's willing to find a new favorite.

Does she think it will happen?

"Yeah. Oh yeah!"

And while the fans cheered for all three, there was no doubt that Wade is still the king of Miami's court.

"There's always gonna be a special place for him," said Daniel Fernandez, 25, as he pointed to the white No. 3 jersey on his chest.

"I've never seen anything like this in basketball," he said. "Three big stars coming together. I'm seeing history!" ■

Even Great Ones Need Help

As Dwyane Wade and LeBron James Can Attest

By Dan Le Batard · June 7, 2011

King-maker Pat Riley tells a story about needing help. Seems that Magic Johnson, ultimate winner, was so short-circuited toward the end of games even with Kareem Abdul-Jabbar's assistance that he didn't want to so much as think. The mental drain of carrying a team against waves of impassioned aggressors, and making all the important decisions, left him fried as the last seconds approached.

Magic wanted to do so little thinking in that weary physical and mental state—"scrambled," to use Riley's word—that he eventually asked his coach to please just hold up easy signs to convey every play he wanted run in the last few minutes. Magic Johnson, leader, floor general, champion, wanted to follow executive orders then, finding a modicum of relief in doing what he was told instead of having to create it all himself. It'll wear you out, making all the decisions from quarter to quarter, game to game, day to day, month to month.

LeBron James and Dwyane Wade grew tired of carrying this kind of late-game cross all alone across several dry seasons and postseasons, James so weary that Cleveland still believes he simply quit at the end of his last broken journey there. It is one of the reasons James and Wade came together, to share that burden, as friends, and make the heavy lifting lighter—the sports equivalent of calling a buddy to help you move a couch. Perhaps you've noticed that 32-year-old Dirk Nowitzki sits in the middle of the very first quarter to keep him fresh for late and that even 22-year-old Derrick Rose rested many more minutes in the last series than the older LeBron. Maybe it is coincidence that Rose didn't have the legs for long jumpers late and James did, but this isn't:

James and Wade do every single interview together, side by side, as symbolic as it is unprecedented, while Rose and Nowitzki are left to endure those postgame questions about not having enough help all alone now. That so many of those questions directed at James and Wade are still about who is the alpha dog/closer is as silly as it is small. They've already answered it again and again, in words and in deeds, against Boston and Chicago and now Dallas, by deciding to come together in the first place and by staying together amid all the turbulence since. They both are, OK? They're both the closer. How many Hall of Famers and MVPs and German gods do you want them to slay before you realize that they don't care whom you credit with the kill?

Dwyane Wade and LeBron James share a laugh at practice during the 2010–2011 season.

Wade high-fives LeBron James after a play during a game against the Bulls in Chicago in the 2011 Eastern Conference finals. Miami beat Chicago 4–1 in the best-of-7 series, making it to the NBA Finals for the second time in franchise history.

It is always interesting how forgetful and short-sighted the dizzying up-and-down of sports can make us, emotion trampling logic. Chris Bosh fixes three horrible games with one timely shot. Wade reinvents/resurrects himself in two games after a playoff series so bad people wondered if he was injured. And now James, after ending all of Boston's Hall of Famers and Chicago's MVP with an avalanche of punctuation points, endures a question about shrinking even in the winning news conference after Game 3.

The way they came together invites this kind of scrutiny and criticism; but being together helps rebut it with a scoreboard's finality. James and Wade saw and felt something we didn't the past few years—something Rose and Nowitzki see and feel clearly now. When you lose, that spotlight goes very fast from warm to scalding.

It is funny, looking back, that the spotlight is the reason nobody believed they would come together in the first place, back when the idea seemed ridiculous. The money, ball, team and late-game glory simply could not and would not be shared by alpha males, not in a bling league and hip-hop culture soaked in gotta-get-mine. The King would not accept even the occasional appearance of being merely a sidekick. The need to be The Man would trump the desire to be The Teammate, The Friend, The Winner and The Champion.

But we've seen this Heat team take a bat to that construct as it shifts basketball's paradigm. Any of these three players can win a game or a series. Bosh was as good against Chicago as he has been bad against Dallas. Wade has been as good against

Dallas as he was bad against Chicago. And if James had been kept out of the paint the way he has in the first three games of this series at another time in his life, he would be down 3–0.

Once upon a time, if Wade or James or Bosh was ever off, their teams simply lost. Now, Bosh can be sloppy for most of the game, James can score two points in the fourth quarter and the Heat still win a pivotal Finals game on the road. The big 30-point games Wade is being celebrated for now, as people rush to make it his team again? He averaged that in last year's playoffs while being extinguished by Boston in five games in the first round.

You want to know why James plays in Miami? You need not watch The Decision television show that wrecked his image. All you need to do is hear Nowitzki and Rose after losing games, the burden solely on them. James didn't want to carry that cross alone anymore. Soon, Chris Paul and Dwight Howard won't, either. In a way, Miami has eased the burden on guys like Nowitzki and Rose. Throwing the ball out of bounds in the last 30 seconds and missing the potential game-winner in Game 3? Nobody blames Nowitzki for being a choker in that spot because they know all he is up against. LeBron closes that game that way, and he gets scorched from sea to shining sea.

Amid all the anger and noise, the Heat's story, at the core, is one of remarkable friends and one of remarkable sharing. That's not how it is seen from the outside, from people rooting for it to collapse like the Heat did in Game 2. Charles Barkley says he saw the Heat trying to play hero ball at the end of that game, Wade and James fighting over the Finals MVP trophy, both of them warring to see who could make the crowd leap up with the kill shot. The Heat is a Rorschach inkblot test. People will see whatever they want, depending on their baggage.

But here is all that matters, and the only thing that has mattered since these three decided to come together:

In Game 3, at a tired time that used to scramble even the great Magic Johnson, as Nowitzki scoured the court for some help, any help, Wade tried to go right against a double-team. There was nothing there. So he shared the ball and the burden with James at the top of the key, who was also double-teamed and decided to share the ball and the burden with a wide-open Bosh. Bosh proceeded to make the game-winner.

On the other end, Nowitzki had that burden all to himself the final 4.4 seconds. He was, as time ticked away and Dallas lost, the only Maverick who touched the ball.

Which might be why Nowitzki says that, yeah, if LeBron James had asked him last offseason, he would have considered teaming up with him, too. ■

Wade goes up for a dunk against the Dallas Mavericks in the 2011 NBA Finals as Mavs forward Dirk Nowitzki looks on.

LeBron James, Dwyane Wade Lead Way

Miami Heat Comes Back in Victory over Indiana Pacers

By Joseph Goodman • May 21, 2012

INDIANAPOLIS—It was the MVP and his long-lost buddy MV3.

Salvaging a series and a season while adding to their legacies, LeBron James and Dwyane Wade combined to score 70 points Sunday in a 101–93 victory against the Indiana Pacers in Game 4 of the Eastern Conference semifinals.

On the brink of falling behind 3–1, the Heat evened the best-of-7 series 2–2 with a pair of epic performances from James and Wade. James, the reigning MVP, finished with 40 points, 18 rebounds, and nine assists.

Wade, who struggled so uncharacteristically in Game 3, responded with a bounce-back game of 30 points, nine rebounds, and six assists.

It was the type of boxscore curators of the Basketball Hall of Fame might one day display in a glass case.

"It was a special performance," said Heat forward Shane Battier. "The series is now 2–2. It's a best-of-3.

"We accomplished what we wanted by getting a split."

The series now shifts back to Miami for Game 5 on Tuesday. Game 6 will be played in Indianapolis on Thursday. Game 7, if necessary, will be played in Miami on Saturday.

After an erratic offensive start by the Heat, James and Wade simply took over the game late in the second quarter. After a pair of free throws by Udonis Haslem with 2:51 left in the first half, James and Wade combined to score the Heat's next 38 points.

For more than 24 minutes—an entire half of basketball—the duo scored every field goal for its team.

"They were tremendous tonight with their force and their will," Heat coach Erik Spoelstra said.

The Heat trailed by 10 points when James delivered a difficult bucket with 3:07 left in the first quarter. From there, he scored nine points in a row to end the first period and then began the process of getting Wade involved in the action.

Just like Game 3, Wade was ice cold in the first quarter. He failed to score the first 12 minutes just as he failed to score in the entire first half in

Dwyane Wade scored 30 points against the Indiana Pacers in Game 4 of the Eastern Conference semifinals, which the Miami Heat won 101–93 to tie the series at two games apiece.

"It was a special performance." —Shane Battier

Game 3. A well-timed assist from James helped change everything—the game's momentum, Wade's confidence and perhaps the entire series.

It came with 43.7 seconds left in the first half, a bounce pass from James to Wade on a back-door cut that finally set Wade's mind at ease. Wade finished the play with a powerful baseline drive-and-dunk to cut the Pacers' lead to five points.

"I told [James] at halftime that I needed that," Wade said.

The duo was just getting started. Wade and James scored 14 points each in the third quarter, and the Heat outscored the Pacers 30–16. Wade was 6 of 6 from the field in the period to go along with four rebounds, an assist and a blocked shot. James was 4 of 7 shooting and 6 of 8 from the foul line in the pivotal third quarter to go along with four rebounds, three assists and two steals.

"You could see the momentum start to turn," James said.

James had 13 rebounds in the second half, including four offensive boards in the fourth quarter alone. He finished the game 14 of 27 from the field and 12 of 16 from the free-throw line. Wade was 10 of 13 shooting in the second half and 13 of 23 from the field overall.

The Heat's third-quarter offensive explosion was a welcome sign for a resurgent team. In the third quarters of Games 2 and 3, Miami combined for 26 points.

"Coming out of the third quarter we just had a sense of urgency to get stops and then we just used what we had it the open court," Wade said. "That's beautiful basketball from the Miami Heat."

Led by 18 boards from James, the Heat outrebounded the Pacers 47–38. James' rebounding total was one shy of a postseason career high. In every game this series, the winning team has won the rebounding battle.

"They killed us on the glass in Game 3," James said. "I felt like I needed to be more aggressive."

Ronny Turiaf started at center for the Heat, but it was Haslem who provided clutch baskets in the fourth quarter. Haslem scored four of the Heat's final five field goals and finished with 14 points and four rebounds.

"He had a warrior's night," Spoelstra said.

Haslem's jumper with 5:56 remaining in the game was the first field goal by a Heat player other than James or Wade since a layup by Joel Anthony with 6:39 left in the second quarter. Mario Chalmers added eight points, including two three-pointers. As a team, the Heat was 5 of 12 from three-point range. ■

After evening up the Eastern Conference semifinals series at 2–2, the Heat routed the Pacers 115–83 in Game 5, behind 28 points from Wade.

Crowned

Heat Wins Second NBA Title Behind Finals MVP LeBron James' Triple-Double

By Joseph Goodman • June 22, 2012

The king finally has his ring.

Two years ago, LeBron James chose to team up with Chris Bosh and Dwyane Wade in Miami and build an instant basketball dynasty. The Heat fell two wins shy of beginning that reign in 2011. On Thursday, Miami's rule over the NBA officially began.

The Heat defeated the Thunder 121–106 at AmericanAirlines Arena in Game 5 of the NBA Finals to clinch the world championship. After losing the first game of the series, the Heat won four in a row to earn the franchise's second NBA championship. Although the Heat's victories in Games 2, 3 and 4 were close and decided by only a few possessions, the clincher was an emphatic statement of basketball greatness.

"We believe we built a team to be around for a while," team president Pat Riley said.

James, named Finals MVP, scored 26 points to go along with 13 assists and 11 rebounds, finishing with a triple-double in the biggest game of his career. His assist total tied a postseason career high. James entered Game 5 averaging 29.3 points, 10 rebounds and six assists in the series.

"It's about damn time," James said after receiving his MVP trophy.

It was a wild ride. A bit of historical perspective: The Heat is the first team in the history of the NBA to win the Finals after trailing in three different series. Miami trailed the Pacers 2–1 in the Eastern Conference semifinals, trailed the Celtics 3–2 in the Eastern Conference finals and trailed the Thunder 1–0 in the Finals.

"We love you, Miami," Spoelstra said. "Thank you for your patience."

James, Wade and Bosh checked out of the game with 3:01 left, and the celebration was on. James smiled and lifted his index finger to the crowd. The building shook with excitement and noise. Minutes later, the celebratory streamers and confetti fell from the rafters, and Spoelstra was drenched with Gatorade.

The entire fourth quarter felt like a coronation inside thunderous AmericanAirlines Arena. The Heat led by 24 points to begin the final period and led by 10 points at halftime.

"Your champion, Miami Heat," NBA commissioner David Stern said during the presentation of the Larry O'Brien Trophy at midcourt.

Led by a barrage of three-pointers, Miami

Dwyane Wade, LeBron James, Chris Bosh, and the rest of the Miami Heat celebrate their 2012 NBA Finals victory in the waning seconds of their 121–106 Game 5 win over the Oklahoma Thunder in Miami on June 21, 2012. The NBA championship was the second for Wade and the Heat, the first for James and Bosh.

blew open the game with a 24–6 run in the third quarter. Battier made two three-pointers during the championship-clinching burst, and Mario Chalmers, Bosh and Mike Miller each had one three-pointer in the run.

Miller, who played with a bad back the entire postseason, was sensational in Game 5. He scored a postseason career-high 23 points and was 7 of 8 from three-point range. The Heat made 14 of 26 attempts from three-point range, setting an NBA Finals record.

Wade had 20 points to go along with eight rebounds and three assists. He and Udonis Haslem now have two championships with the Heat. Haslem had one point, one assist, and one rebound in Game 5.

"Since I won it six years ago, I've been through a lot in my personal life and I've been through a lot in my professional life," Wade said. "This one means so much more."

Bosh, who missed nine consecutive games during the playoffs with an abdominal strain, had 24 points and seven rebounds. His three-pointer with 3:30 left in the third quarter gave the Heat a 25-point lead. Miller expanded the lead to 28 points with a three-pointer on the Heat's next possession.

"We came here to win a championship, and we got it done," Bosh said.

James, whose postseason performance will enter the pantheon of the sport, did it with force and might, throwing his 6-8, 250-pound frame at the rim for four rounds. He scored at least 16 points in the lane in each of his final seven playoff games. It was the longest such streak of his career.

Setting a new standard for postseason greatness, James had 13 games in the playoffs with at least 25 points, five rebounds and five assists. Michael Jordan, Larry Bird and James held the old record of 11 consecutive games with at least 25–5–5 in the postseason.

The Heat broke off a 10–2 run early in the third quarter to push its lead to double digits. Chalmers drained his second three-pointer of the game less than two minutes into the quarter, and Battier followed with his second triple.

Led by James' urgency, the Heat began the game like a team ready to close out the series. James started the scoring with a soaring dunk and then slashed to the basket for a five-point burst midway through the period. Bosh matched James' aggression in the lane, and Miller emerged from the bench to provide his most significant contribution of the series.

Miller, who played throughout the entire postseason with a bad back, literally limped into the game in the first quarter. He then started stroking three-pointers, including two that were back-to-back.

Miller had more points (nine) by halftime than he had in the series' first four games combined (eight).

Shane Battier finished with 11 points and was 3 of 7 from three-point range. Chalmers had 10 points and was 2 of 4 from three-point range.

Kevin Durant led the Thunder with 23 points, and Russell Westbrook had 19. The Heat shot 51.9 percent from the field and 53.8 percent from three-point range, and the Thunder shot 41.4 percent.

"We're going to have a party tonight," Riley said. ◼

Wade goes up for a layup in the 2012 NBA Finals against Oklahoma as Thunder guard James Harden watches. The Miami guard averaged 22.6 points in the 4–1 series victory for the Heat.

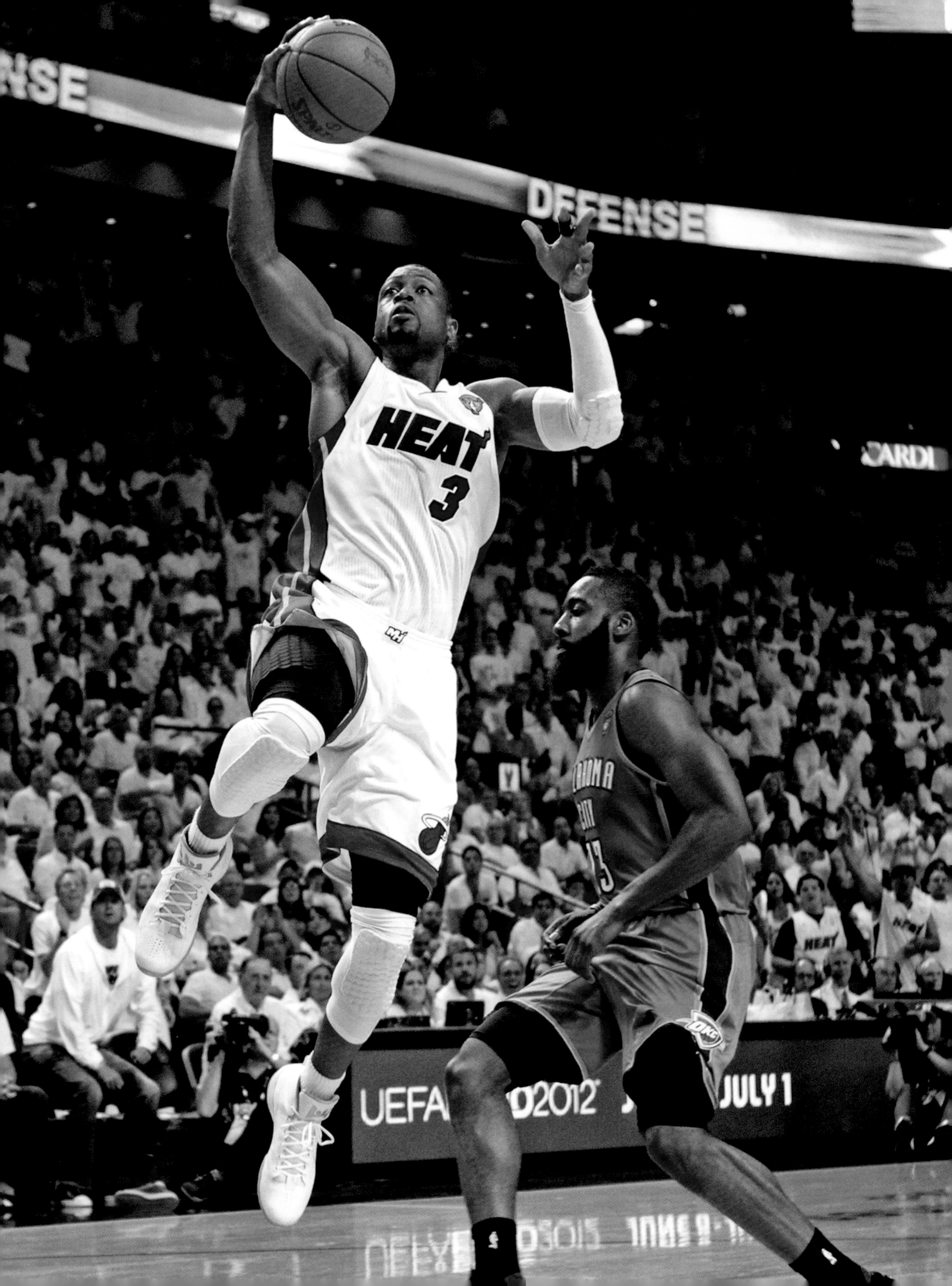
DEFENSE
HEAT
3
JULY 1

More Than Just a Flash of Greatness

Dwyane Wade Knows More Is Needed for Miami Heat Success

By Joseph Goodman · June 15, 2013

SAN ANTONIO—For several years now, Dwyane Wade has shunned his old nickname and asked teammates, reporters, and fans to strike it from their memories. You know the one. It rhymes with slash.

There is a widely understood rule inside and outside of the Heat's locker room that Wade has prohibited people from calling him Flash, which he says he left in his past and which no longer properly describes a more mature version of himself.

Well, forget all that nonsense. Mike Miller, not exactly a rule follower, couldn't help himself Thursday night during Game 4 of the NBA Finals. Like an excited fan, Miller randomly screamed "Flash" in Wade's general direction throughout his resurgent throwback performance. Wade's effort, buoyed by 33 points from LeBron James and 20 from Chris Bosh, allowed the Heat to tie the best-of-7 NBA Finals at 2–2, ensuring at least one game back in Miami.

Wade, who scored 32 points, joined Hall of Famer Isiah Thomas as the only players in NBA Finals history to score at least 30 points while recording six steals.

Flashy indeed—kind of like all those crazy postgame outfits Wade always wears, only better.

"I needed a game like this, but my teammates needed a game like this from me—needed me to be aggressive; needed me to play the way that I'm capable of," said Wade, who has now scored at least 32 points in a NBA Finals game seven times in his career. "Most important, they needed the Big 3 to play the way we're capable of. We're not going to win this series if myself, Chris, and LeBron don't show up to play on a consistent basis.

"So [Thursday night] was kind of one of the best performances that we all had in the playoffs together at the same time. Just being aggressive from start to finish, and hopefully that's what we can see for the next three games."

Like everyone else, it appears Wade is already preparing for the Finals to go seven games. The Heat hasn't won two in a row in 10 games now, but Miami will need to link two victories together to earn its third championship in franchise history.

In other words, Wade might need to embrace

Dwyane Wade finishes off a dunk with style in Game 4 of the 2013 NBA Finals versus the San Antonio Spurs. Wade finished with 32 points, six rebounds, four assists and six steals, and the Miami Heat won 109–93, to even the series at 2–2.

"He has proven his toughness, and he doesn't want to talk about his health....He's giving us everything he has." —Erik Spoelstra

his inner Flash a few more times. He was averaging less than 15 points per game in the postseason before his vintage performance in Game 4, which reminded anyone with eyes of his epic effort in the 2006 Finals. After falling behind the Mavericks 2–0, the Heat won four in a row with Wade scoring 42, 36, 43 and 36 points in consecutive games.

Wade, with his injured right knee, was always the X factor going into these Finals and, considering the injury, James called Wade's effort in Game 4 "amazing."

Consider this: Wade scored 18 points in the second half of Game 4. That's more than double the points he scored in the second halves of Games 1, 2 and 3 combined (eight). For the first time this postseason, Wade kept his knee loose during breaks in the action—between quarters and during substitutions—by wrapping hot packs around his knee. The treatment method now likely will be repeated throughout the rest of the Finals.

Another slight change: Wade said playing more minutes actually helped. He logged 40 minutes in Game 4 after averaging just 33 minutes in the first three games of the Finals. Wade has called his injury a deep bone bruise, but the pain has lingered for months.

"I felt the last couple of times when I went to the bench I stiffened up a little bit," Wade said. "I tried to keep myself loose and tried to work with [coach Erik Spoelstra] on not sitting me so long. You know, coming out when I get tired and getting back in there a little quicker and trying to keep my body going and moving."

In a conference call Friday, Spoelstra didn't go into too much detail about the specifics of Wade's injury, saying Wade would be "disappointed" if his coach used the injury as an excuse. But Spoelstra did add some weight to Wade's performance by acknowledging that the Heat shooting guard "really should be commended that he's out there."

"He has proven his toughness, and he doesn't want to talk about his health," Spoelstra said. "But, hey, he's willing to go out there and compete for his teammates and open himself up for criticism with expectations of something bigger. And he's giving us everything he has.

"And [Thursday night] he was able to dig deeper and go to another place that we needed. Sometimes it changes from game to game. But he understood he had to have a major impact on the game [Thursday night] in a lot of different ways. And he did it. That was pretty impressive." ■

Wade averaged 19.6 points per game during the Heat's 4–3 NBA Finals victory over the Spurs. He shot .476 from the field in helping secure Miami's and the Big 3's second straight NBA championship.

Dwyane Wade's Unselfish Attitude

What Allowed the Big 3 Era to Happen for Miami Heat

By Greg Cote · June 26, 2013

All of this started with Micky Arison, the franchise owner, and his checkbook, his willingness to put his money where his dream was.

All of this started with Pat Riley, the club president and builder, and his vision, his audacity to conceive this blueprint and then go get it.

All of this started with LeBron James, the incomparable player, and his sublime excellence, then his decision to take it "to South Beach."

This, in many ways, is the Heat's real Big 3: the moneyman, the architect, and the singular talent. You could argue that these are the three most indispensable men in the grand plan that has fashioned two championship parades in a row so far.

And you would be right, to a point.

Except there was a fourth man without whom none of this would have happened.

Not Arison's riches nor Riley's recruiting would have landed LeBron if not for the willingness and sacrifice of Dwyane Wade.

His mind-set, around this time in 2010, was the seed from which all this grew—a fact worth celebrating right along with the championship parades that Wade, in effect, allowed to happen.

He could have blown up all of this before it ever materialized, if he let his ego get in the way, if his main consideration was himself, not the greater good.

"If I was selfish, then this team would never have been assembled," Wade admits. "Then, with this team assembled, if I was selfish, it never would have worked."

It worked—famously—because Wade was able to see that championship rings and parades were more important than his own status as the unequivocal face of the franchise. He understood that James was the one player in the NBA who was an in-his-prime megastar, a bigger national star than Wade himself.

Wade had been the 2006 Finals MVP. He had won a league scoring title. He had made All-NBA first teams. He had established himself individually in a certain Hall of Fame career to a degree that proved his talent, his brand. Had he not, perhaps his welcoming LeBron would not

Dwyane Wade doesn't even have to look to know that LeBron James will finish off his assist during a 2010–2011 regular-season game against the Milwaukee Bucks.

After the Miami Heat's Game 7 win over the San Antonio Spurs in the 2013 NBA Finals, the Big 3 celebrate their second straight NBA championship, the Heat's and Wade's third, James' and Bosh's second.

have been as easy—not that it was easy.

It took Wade that first year to get to the point of acknowledging the new hierarchy, of adjusting to it. Once he did, and stepped aside so LeBron could step forward, the championships started coming.

Magic Johnson, in town with the ABC broadcast crew for the Finals, last week called Wade "the most unselfish superstar I've ever seen in my life," adding, "No superstar would do what Dwyane did."

Riley has said the same.

Wade's personal friendship with LeBron that predated their becoming teammates made Wade's sacrifice easier. So did the fact Dwyane knew LeBron was all about winning championships, too.

When James said the night of Finals Game 7, "Coming through for my teammates and not letting them down makes me more satisfied than anything in the world"—that was the LeBron that Wade had known all along.

At some point great players understand that championships ultimately distinguish them more than individual statistics.

That's why Wade began his postgame news conference on that champagne-kissed night by jokingly saying he wanted to be referred to from now on not as Dwyane, but as "Three"—not for his uniform number, but for the number of his NBA championships.

Earlier, without the crush of media on him, Wade—Three—had been on his back making snow angels in the confetti on the court. Later he had been sitting on the floor outside the locker room, cigar in hand, not speaking, simply ruminating.

"We go through life so fast. The championships I've won seemed like they went past me so fast," he would say later of that solitary interlude. "I wanted to take a minute, take a moment and just soak in being a kid from Robbins, Illinois, from Marquette and now having three championships. To get to the Finals three years in a row and win two is unbelievable."

Championships are like children. You are supposed to love them all equally, but each is special in its way.

"This is the sweetest one by far because of everything we've been through, everything I've been through individually," Wade said.

Three deep bone bruises in his right knee had been treated with plasma therapy. The other knee was injured during the Finals, requiring seven hours of treatment—including a fluid-drain prior to Game 7.

His right knee had been hurting a month before

Wade dishes off to a Heat teammate during Game 3 of the 2013 NBA Finals versus the Spurs in San Antonio.

the postseason even began, and playing continually aggravated the injury. He wouldn't talk about it. It was there as a crutch for him, an excuse, but he wouldn't use it.

Bulls star Derrick Rose, medically cleared to play, cautiously sat out the entire postseason, babying his knee.

Wade could have done the same, but didn't.

Instead, for much of the playoffs his scoring was down, and the critics were out. Was he past his prime? An ESPN.com article even suggested he should be benched.

"They tried to bury Dwyane, but he kept pushing open the coffin door," said teammate Shane Battier. "And that's Dwyane Wade. You can't really define him by stats. He's a competitor, a fighter. When it counts most, he'll be there."

Wade would score 23 points with 10 rebounds and two blocked shots in the ultimate Game 7, including important late baskets that padded Miami's leads to 81–75 and 90–85.

"He was in attack mode," described LeBron. "At that point you knew this was the D-Wade we've all wanted to see."

Wade ran to Spurs coach Gregg Popovich seconds after the game ended to congratulate him on the season. He said "Pop" told him, "You were Dwyane Wade tonight."

Only the men in his own locker room knew how limited Wade had been by the knees.

"We knew what he was dealing with," coach Erik Spolestra said. "Really, he should be commended for being out there at all and doing whatever it takes, putting himself out there for

criticism because he wasn't 100 percent. It was a selfless effort for two months. Some players wouldn't have played."

Wade said he felt better during the Finals than in previous playoff rounds. Come Game 7, he knew he had to be his old self.

"I'm about gutting it out," Wade said. "I talked to my knees. We had a conversation. I told them, I said, 'Listen both of you guys, if y'all can give me one great game, you'll have a great summer.' So I'm going to treat my knees very well this summer and rest them."

Wade could not help but revel a bit in satisfaction after his 23-point Game 7 had helped secure the franchise's third championship.

He had earned the right.

"My belief is stronger than your doubt," Wade had said, of his critics and doubters in general. "I'm always going to believe. When it's a big game, I don't care what I'm going through, No. 3 is going to show up. He's going to do something to help his team win."

Ten years after he first appeared here, drafted out of Marquette, it might be time to finally wonder if Wade has surpassed Dolphins icon Dan Marino—or should—as our single greatest professional athlete.

Hall of Fame credentials and 10 seasons of growing into a beloved local figure make a pretty good argument.

Maybe the argument ender, though, is the sacrifice Dwyane Wade made—personally and professionally—that allowed the Big 3 era and these championships to happen. ■

Healthy Dwyane Wade Working Wonders for Miami Heat

By Joseph Goodman · May 24, 2014

It doesn't work without Dwyane Wade.

Those were LeBron James' words before the start of this season. For six months, they served as a constant reminder of how much gravity was resting atop Wade's shoulders as his knees rested on the Heat's bench.

With three championships in a row as the goal and with options on their contracts after this postseason, those knees needed to work in the playoffs.

They have.

Not only has Wade played his part in these Eastern Conference finals, he also has outplayed James and provided some much-needed consistency to the lineup while James dithered defensively in Game 1 and twiddled offensively for three quarters in Game 2.

There have been plenty of times in the past three years when Wade has been thankful to be on the same team as James, but the pecking order has been flipped with Game 3 of this best-of-7 series on Saturday.

Lately, James should be grateful to be on a team with Wade. On Friday, Wade demanded more.

"For us, we haven't played as well as we want to yet," Wade said. "We have other levels that we have to reach. We have to get to that level where we're playing Miami Heat basketball. You guys know how that looks when we're all on one court, and we're all playing together.

"So we have a lot more improvement we could do in this series."

The series is tied 1–1, and the Heat now has home-court advantage. But James hasn't played his best basketball. For the two-time defending champions, that's a position of strength. James is averaging 23.5 points per game and shooting 20 percent (2 of 10) from three-point range. Wade's numbers have been phenomenal: 25 points per game and 64.7 percent shooting from the field.

"We figured out a way to win the ball game on the road, when they had control of it coming down [the] last three, four minutes," Wade said of Game 2 in Indianapolis. "So that was a good team finding

Miami Heat guard Dwyane Wade raises his arms during Game 2 of the Eastern Conference semifinals against the Brooklyn Nets, which the Heat won 94–82 to go up 2–0 in the best-of-7 series.

a way to win on the road versus another good team, but I don't feel like we've played our best basketball."

After a regular season dedicated to remaining healthy, Wade continues to improve physically as the Heat progresses through the postseason.

He carried the Heat to victory in Game 5 against the Brooklyn Nets in the Eastern Conference semifinals, and he was the team's most reliable offensive threat on Tuesday in Game 2 of the Eastern Conference finals. Wade led the Heat with 23 points and was at his best at the beginning and end of the pivotal victory. There were plenty of questions surrounding the Heat's longtime star entering the playoffs, but he has answered them so far.

Wade was 8 of 10 combined in the first and fourth quarters of Game 2, and he had 10 of the Heat's 25 points in the final period. His prominent role in the Heat's most important game of the postseason through the first three rounds added further proof that Wade is still one of the best shooting guards in the NBA. Wade missed 28 games during the regular season, and that maintenance program has helped the 32-year-old guard grow stronger through the playoffs.

"That was the plan," Wade said. "I just want to continue it—just want to get better. There's a lot of basketball left, but I feel good."

Wade's 23 points in Game 2 were a postseason high against the Pacers over the past two years. He averaged just 15.4 points against the Pacers in the 2013 Eastern Conference finals while struggling with chronic tendonitis in his knees. In the Heat's 2012 series against the Pacers, Wade

had fluid drained from his knee and at one point had to be removed from a team huddle to avoid a confrontation with Heat coach Erik Spoelstra.

Wade struggled throughout the 2013 playoffs with knee soreness and even produced a documentary to chronicle his struggles. In the offseason, Wade underwent OssaTron shockwave therapy to help strengthen his knees. The estimated full recovery time on that procedure was six months, and it appears Wade and the Heat's training staff timed his recovery perfectly.

Of course, the best indication of Wade's improving health perhaps was when his knee accidentally collided with the back of Paul George's head in the fourth quarter of Game 2. Wade was slow to get up and limped off the court during a timeout, but he returned to finish the fourth quarter and even appeared to have a little more life in his legs than James late in the game.

James missed a breakaway layup with 3:18 left in the game, but Wade was there to clean up the miss with a putback dunk.

"Usually, D-Wade don't even chase me down," James said. "He knows if it's a one-on-one matchup with me, most of the time I'm going to score. I was glad he did. Huge momentum play in the fourth quarter when we needed it most."

Said Wade: "Like he said, 99.9 percent of the time, when he's one-on-one with someone, we take our chances. Just at that moment, I actually noticed he didn't really get the acceleration like he needed. He took a step and didn't get up.

"Normally he explodes, and there's not many people that can meet him at the top. He didn't

Wade's health rebounded in 2013–2014, when he averaged 19 points per game on .545 shooting from the field during the regular season. In the 2014 postseason, he averaged 17.8 points with a .500 field-goal percentage.

get the explosion on the layup that he needed."

The field goal gave the Heat a five-point lead, and Wade followed up that play with a steal seconds later on a bad pass by George. Wade guarded George, the Pacers' best player, in the fourth quarter and limited him to six points.

"Dwyane has been one of the finer, more dynamic two-way players in this league for a long time," Spoelstra said.

"He understands that as well as anybody that you can impact a win on both sides of the court. So, that's not only creating the offense for us on the other end, it's taking a challenge on one of the best scorers in the league."

Wade then secured a key offensive rebound with 2:41 to play following a missed three-pointer by James. Wade later finished the possession with a five-foot jumper.

Then, following a tip-in by center Roy Hibbert on the Pacers' next possession, Wade's 18-foot jumper gave the Heat a seven-point lead with 1:37 to play.

Like an exclamation mark at the end of his statement game, Wade's reverse dunk with 21.6 seconds remaining started the celebration for his teammates on the bench. Wade scored eight points in a row for the Heat during the game's final two minutes. ■

Dethroned

Miami Heat's Threepeat Bid Thwarted

By Joseph Goodman · June 15, 2014

SAN ANTONIO—It was a heck of a run.

If the Heat just provided Miami and South Florida with their greatest sports dynasty, it was a thrill from beginning to end. Led by LeBron James, Dwyane Wade and Chris Bosh, the Heat has reached four consecutive NBA Finals, won two in a row and given fans something to celebrate summer after summer after summer after summer.

This might not be the end of James' Heat, of course, but the championship-winning streak came to a convincing end at San Antonio's AT&T Center on Sunday night. The Spurs defeated the two-time defending champions 104–87 in Game 5 to win the 2014 NBA Finals. Bosh called this year's version of the Spurs the best team he has ever played against, and James and Wade agreed.

"They dominated us in every facet," James said.

James began Game 5 with one of his classic offensive tears, scoring 17 points in the first quarter, but the NBA Finals MVP in 2012 and 2013 didn't get as much support from Bosh and Wade this time, and an avalanche of Spurs' offense was simply too much to overcome. After the first quarter, the Spurs outscored the Heat 82–58 to close out the best-of-7 series 4–1.

James finished with 31 points, going 10 of 21 from the field, 3 of 9 from three-point range, and 8 of 9 from the free-throw line. The Heat's other starters combined to score just 32 points. Ray Allen started in place in Mario Chalmers, but that wrinkle didn't make much of a difference. Allen finished with five points, and Chalmers had eight points off the bench.

"It's been a hell of a ride in these four years," Wade said.

Wade scored 11 points, and Bosh had 13. Starter Rashard Lewis finished with three points.

"It's somewhat still disbelief, but because it was such a great team it really makes it worth it for us," said a gracious Spurs coach Gregg Popovich. "It's just great satisfaction beating such a great team. They're a class act and they'll be back next year for sure. I don't think anyone would really doubt that."

Wherever the Heat's future goes from here— only reserve guard Norris Cole is locked in contractually for next season—team president Pat Riley's grand experiment should be considered a huge success. The team has reached the NBA Finals every season since James and Bosh joined Wade.

"As painful as it feels right now, you have to have perspective," Heat coach Erik Spoelstra said.

Dwyane Wade passes the ball while being guarded by the Spurs' Tim Duncan during the 2014 NBA Finals in San Antonio.

"Even the team we were playing against has never made it to four straight Finals. You can't be jaded enough to not appreciate that. None of us really feel those emotions right now, but at some point this summer hopefully we can step back and gain some perspective about this. It takes a special group."

The Heat's magical comeback against the Spurs in 2013 was considered one of the best Finals in NBA history, but the rematch never came close to matching that drama. The Spurs got their revenge without much fuss.

"You have to absolutely credit their offense," Spoelstra said. "It was exquisite basketball with ball movement and player movement and unselfish basketball."

Popovich's team went nearly a full calendar year fueled by the belief that it gave away the 2013 NBA Finals to the Heat. After trouncing the Heat in Games 3 and 4 of the series in Miami, the Spurs closed out the Eastern Conference champions with ease. Spurs forward Kawhi Leonard, now in his third season in the NBA, emerged during the series as a budding superstar. He led the Spurs in scoring in Game 3, 4 and 5, and had 22 points in Sunday's championship-clinching victory. Leonard went 7 of 10 from the field, 3 of 4 from three-point range, and 5 of 6 from the free-throw line and was named the series' MVP during the trophy presentation.

"He listens, he's a great learner, and he's super competitive, and he has the drive to be the best, and it's really uncommon," Popovich said of Leonard. "He walks the walk. He's there early, and he's there late."

Reserve Manu Ginobili was a force off the bench. He scored 19 points and provided the Spurs with the best highlight of the series when the drove through the lane and dunked over Bosh in the second quarter.

Ginobili followed with a three-pointer to cap the Spurs' comeback.

The Heat gave the Spurs the best it had in the first half, but it simply wasn't enough.

After that, the Heat was done.

Miami held the Spurs to just three points in the first four minutes of the second half, but that effort came with a major caveat. The Heat couldn't score either, and went the first four minutes of the second half without any points.

A driving layup by Bosh gave the Heat its first basket of the third quarter with 7:53 remaining in the period. That's when the Spurs started pouring it on.

San Antonio reeled off six consecutive points, and a reverse layup by reserve Patty Mills gave the Spurs a 56–42 lead with 6:36 left in the period. The Heat called a timeout to quell the Spurs' momentum, and that's when it got worse. So much worse.

The Spurs outscored the Heat 30–18 in the third quarter with Mills going 4 of 4 from three-point range. Mills had 14 points in the period and finished with 17 overall. Tony Parker scored 14 points for the Spurs, and Tim Duncan had 14.

The Spurs had just eight turnovers and held the Heat to 40 percent shooting from the field and 28 percent shooting (7 of 25) from three-point range.

A relentless effort by James helped give the Heat a 29–22 lead after the first quarter.

James played all but 14 seconds in the first period and scored 17 points. It gave the Heat a 29–22 lead after the first quarter, but that didn't last long. Allen's three-pointer in the first period tied for Chalmers' total number of three-pointers in the series, but Wade and Bosh had trouble finding their rhythms. That was a problem in the second quarter.

The Spurs outscored the Heat 25–11 in the period. James couldn't carry the Heat for every minute of the first half, and Bosh and Wade weren't up to the challenge.

"I just struggled a bit," Wade said. "I'm never going to point at anything physically. I felt fine. I just struggled a little bit offensively. You know, I wish I could have done more, but it's the nature [of the] game, you know." ■

Dwyane Wade, LeBron James, Chris Bosh, and center Chris Andersen (left) look on as their threepeat hopes fade during their 2014 NBA Finals loss to the San Antonio Spurs, four games to one. The defeat ended a streak of four straight Finals appearances, and two NBA championships in a row for Miami and the Big 3.

Wade off the Court and in the Community

Opposite: Dwyane Wade at his D. Wade All-Star Basketball Camp at Nova Southeastern University's University Center in July 2011.

Above: Gabrielle Union and Wade serve at the 23rd annual Heat Thanksgiving Celebration at the Miami Rescue Mission in November 2014. Wade and Union are known as one of the most notable and generous couples in both the sports and entertainment worlds.

Opposite: Gabrielle Union gets help fitting her helmet before taking off in the D.Wade Community Bike Ride at Regatta Park in Coconut Grove in September 2016. Dwyane Wade led the six-mile bike ride, which aimed to bring the community together.

Below: Wade stands with Union (left) and his mother, Jolinda (right) on the "white carpet" during a fundraiser at a private home in March 2012 in Coral Gables.

Messy Breakup

A Sad, Traumatic Ending to Wade's Epic Miami Story

By Dan Le Batard · July 7, 2016

So cruel sometimes, the emotions business. Dwyane Wade leaves Miami now, all wrong, and the people who care deeply, too deeply, unreasonably deeply, will argue and yell about where the blame should go for that. It will be passionate and hurt and angry, but then that will exhaust itself, and you know what will take its place? Sadness. Deep, awful, empty, dark sadness that feels a lot like a sickness in the bones. Sports, man.

Heat fans. Pat Riley. Wade himself. They will all feel this sadness and mourn how they botched the ending, and they will remember the best times with nostalgia and stinging eyes, and it'll leave them hollowed out like all of the best relationships fresh from breakup. Those were good times, man. So, so good. It might have been the right time for all of them to move on, given how they felt about each other at the end, but it can be hard to see clearly through the rage and grief and tears of the present. It was a really great and healthy relationship…right up until it wasn't.

How mad and wounded and disrespected and taken for granted and distrustful must you feel to do what Wade just did?

To throw away your blessed relationship with a city and the only professional workplace you've ever known for an offer that wasn't much better than Miami's?

Wade is the most beloved athlete South Florida has ever had, its greatest champion. He brought Shaquille O'Neal his last championship as a center, and Riley his last championship as a coach. He owns more rings than the Dolphins. More rings than the Marlins. He helped bring his friend, LeBron James, to us, and created the most interesting team this city has ever known. His Hall of Fame résumé is soaked in sparkles and proves he is about as good at what he did as anyone has ever been at anything.

South Florida watched him grow up, from the kid who needed student-loan help for his kid's diapers at Marquette to an international icon. Saw him get divorced, write a book about fatherhood, marry a Hollywood starlet, become a businessman. We saw him age before our eyes, from a baby-faced, fast-twitch acrobat who could get 25 free throws in an NBA Finals game to a savvy, slower killer who finished the last season Charlotte played.

This ending, though, it feels like watching your kid trip and fall off the graduation stage. Miami tried to keep him. But not enough for his liking,

Dwyane Wade hugs teammate Goran Dragić after the Miami Heat's 103–91 win over the Toronto Raptors in Game 6 of the Eastern Conference semifinals, Wade's last game at Miami's AmericanAirlines Arena before signing with the Chicago Bulls after the end of the season. The Heat was eliminated from the playoffs two days later by a Game 7 loss in Toronto.

"He will always be a part of us." —Pat Riley

clearly, and not enough to mortgage its future to repay him for his past. Riley talks a lot about family, but the mafia is a family, too, and the godfather wasn't going to handcuff his flexibility to do his job in the future by tying himself emotionally to an aging star whose percentages are all in decline. This wasn't about money, rest assured. Chicago gave Wade approximately $47 million, but Miami's $41.5 million final offer (all its remaining salary-cap space) was about the same once you throw in Florida's lack of state income tax.

Wade felt unwanted, for whatever his reasons. Wade felt underappreciated, for whatever his reasons. That'll all come out soon enough. His relationship with Riley was in tatters by the end, damaged by the way Wade's allegiances always seemed to be to LeBron James. The Heat's proud reputation as loyalty lifers takes a hit today as its prodigal son leaves behind all the warmth in his past for a cold Chicago. Ego and pride and willfulness and stubbornness—some of the things that helped make him a champion—also made him pack his bags and move out.

Riley was too raw to talk about it Wednesday night, but I asked him if he wanted to say anything about how he was feeling, and this is what he wrote by text:

"SADDDDDDD!!!! SO saddddddd! I will never forget the sixth game in Dallas in 2006. DW rebounded the ball, and threw it to the heavens and the Heat universe was perfect for that moment. Our first world championship. Our universe is not perfect today. It will be fraught with anger, judgment, blame instead of THANK YOU!!! Ten years ago. Ten years older. Ten years wiser. Ten years changed. All of us. Dwyane had a choice, and he made it. He went home. Bad, bad summer for us. But there will be another 10 years, and it will be someone or something else in 2026. Move on with no blood or tears. Just thanks. I truly loved Dwyane, but families grow, change and get on with another life. He will always be a part of us. ALWAYS! And no more bruises and enough fighting. Let's just fly above it if we can and never forget. I feel his pain and pride for what pushed him over the ledge. Been there. Forever, for always, your coach I will be. FOREVER!"

As Junot Diaz wrote in *This Is How You Lose Her*, "And that's when I knew it was over. As soon as you start thinking about the beginning, it's the end." Maggi Richard may have put it better: "Two words. Three vowels. Four consonants. Seven letters. It can either cut you open to the core and leave you in ungodly pain or it can free your soul and lift a tremendous weight off your shoulders. The phrase is: It's over."

Riley plays for championships, not No. 3 seeds. So he was in a bit of a no-win position once he swung big and missed on Kevin Durant. Lose Wade, and your team loses. Keep Wade, and your

team isn't good enough, either, especially not with what Golden State is doing. But, man, that felt like it collapsed quickly somehow, even though we've been seeing the warnings for two years, like watching an old Las Vegas casino being dynamited. Miami went from the most interesting team in sports—LeBron James, Wade, Chris Bosh— to suddenly having immature nomad Hassan Whiteside as its healthiest face. And this might all get messier for Miami if the organization decides to fight to keep Bosh off the court to clear his salary space by February so it can better go after the big free agent class of 2017 that will include LeBron, Durant, Steph Curry, Blake Griffin, Chris Paul and Russell Westbrook.

Some crushed kids lost their sports innocence Wednesday night. Some adults threw temper tantrums like crushed kids. Riley, the old legend, looks lost as he searches for his ending and an older Wade, wounded, limps off toward his ending in all the wrong colors and feelings.

Breakups hurt, man. ■

Wade sits on the bench next to Chris Bosh during a 2015–2016 regular-season game against the Milwaukee Bucks. The Heat went 48–34, finishing third in the Eastern Conference—a far cry from their Big 3 glory days with LeBron James, who left two years prior to rejoin the Cleveland Cavaliers.

Dwyane Wade's Return to Miami Filled with Cheers, Emotional Moments

By Manny Navarro • November 11, 2016

When he pulled up to AmericanAirlines Arena on Thursday evening, it didn't take long for Dwyane Wade to get the kind of reception he became accustomed to for 13 seasons.

Arena workers greeted him with applause, high fives, and hugs before the Golden Oldies dancers saw him and began cheering loudly. Eventually, Wade found his way to the visitors' locker room.

"It felt normal until I pulled up and I went to the opposite side of the building—I absolutely did not know where to go," said Wade, who slept in his Miami home Wednesday night for the first time since leaving to begin camp with the Chicago Bulls in late September.

"It was just a little different walk into the arena. But it was great to walk in and see familiar faces right away."

Wade's return to the city he called home for 13 seasons was filled with plenty of warm, inviting moments.

It started when he jogged out onto the court with his Chicago Bulls teammates to a standing ovation and then continued when stadium announcer Mike Baiamonte introduced him like he has for 13 years—even though now he's playing for the other team.

Wade, 34, received a standing ovation after his initial introduction. Fans chanted "D-Wade!" Those cheers only got louder after he made his first basket—an eight-foot runner on his fourth shot of the game with 7:02 to play in the opening quarter—and then grew to a fever pitch when, during the first timeout of the game, a two-minute tribute video for Wade played on the big screens inside the arena.

When the montage was over, Wade walked out onto the court, arms raised and thanked the fans. Owner Micky Arison and team president Pat Riley stood and applauded in their usual seats courtside.

About an hour and a half before tip-off, Riley told a handful of local reporters he finally did send Wade the long, carefully crafted email he had been

Chicago Bulls guard Dwyane Wade acknowledges the fans at AmericanAirlines Arena in Miami after a tribute video to Wade played during a timeout in the game against the Heat on November 10, 2016. It was Wade's first game back in Miami after signing with his hometown Bulls in the offseason.

talking about since Wade first left in July. Riley, though, didn't specify when exactly it was he sent it to Wade. Prior to Wade's return Thursday, the two most influential people in Heat history had not spoken since Miami was eliminated in the playoffs last May.

"I hope he got it," Riley said about 90 minutes before tip-off. "You know those guys changing phone numbers and emails…"

Wade said he did.

"I haven't spoken to Pat since I got into the building. I really haven't had time," Wade said during his pregame press conference with the biggest media crowd the Heat has attracted all season. "I did look at my emails today. I got emails from him. I didn't have time to read them yet. I'll take time on the plane somewhere to read them.

"There's nothing to squash, in my eyes," Wade said of his relationship with Riley. "I've spoken to you guys and he's heard me very loud and clear. I'm just appreciative of Pat and what he helped me—what we created together here in Miami."

Wade said he was going to take a moment during the singing of the national anthem Thursday to stand and stare at some of those accomplishments. While Miami's three championship banners hang for everyone in the arena to see, for 13 years they were at Wade's back during the anthem. Thursday was the first time Wade said he was going to be able to stand in front of him.

"A lot of memories, man," Wade said. "Got some good memories, man, got some bad ones too—some injuries. But all good from the standpoint how everything happened for me and my career here in my 13 years. I wouldn't change it for the world. It was spectacular, and I couldn't get on my knees and ask God for a better pro career and the start or the finish of it. I'm proud of it."

Now, though, he's proud to be playing back in the city where he grew up—Chicago. Asked about it Thursday, Wade said he isn't thinking about his future beyond this season (he signed a two-year, $47 million deal with the Bulls this summer with a player option for the 2017–18 season).

What Wade admits he does still think often about are his former Heat teammates. He said he watches every Heat game he can and said he's oftened called his old friend and teammate Udonis Haslem after Miami's losses to talk to him "about how they could have won those games."

"I'm not a hateful individual at all. I root for their success," Wade said of the Heat. "I want to see how Tyler [Johnson] does. I want to see how Justise [Winslow] is growing. I want to see Hassan [Whiteside] be Hassan, be a beast on the floor. I want to see him shut everybody up that [doesn't] think he's going to continue to play the way he plays because he got paid. I want UD to get in and be old reliable UD. I root for those guys."

"He gave us a great 13 years, three [championship] rings, Olympic gold medalist," Haslem said of Wade before delivering his punchline with a big smile on his face. "Behind me, he's probably the second best player in the history of the organization." ■

Wade scored 13 points, with seven rebounds and four assists in the Bulls' 98–95 victory over the Heat.

He's Back!

Cleveland Trades Dwyane Wade Back to the Miami Heat

By Jordan McPherson, Barry Jackson and Manny Navarro · February 8, 2018

Dwyane Wade is coming home. The guard who helped lead Miami to three championships was traded by the Cleveland Cavaliers to the Heat on Thursday, as first reported by ESPN and confirmed by a source.

The Heat acquired Wade in exchange for a heavily protected future second-round pick.

Whereas the Cavaliers were looking to get younger and more athletic, the Heat had three reasons to trade for Wade:

- Miami needed help at shooting guard, with Dion Waiters out for the season and Tyler Johnson struggling.
- The price to get him was modest—a second-round pick. He's making only the $2.3 million league minimum, less than $1.1 million prorated for the remainder of the season.
- According to a source, the Heat wanted to end things the right way with Wade after he left the franchise in a contract dispute in the summer of 2016.

Wade, 36, is still effective; he is averaging 11.2 points on 45.5 percent shooting.

Heat players were stunned to learn of the trade after practice.

"Are you joking or are you for real?" Hassan Whiteside asked.

"D-Waaaaaaaaaaade! I definitely got more lobs when D-Wade was around. His IQ is amazing. I don't know what we traded for him, but come on back, D-Wade. Great news for me. Great news, in my eyes."

Johnson said: "I couldn't imagine us getting him back like this, but I'll take a Hall of Famer. You know Wade County and all that. I think it's going to help UD [Udonis Haslem] the most. He finally has another voice with someone who has won and played at the highest level. This is his franchise. Bringing him back is going to rejuvinate a lot of things. I think it's an uplifting thing."

Before last Wednesday's Heat-Cavaliers game, Wade said he wanted to finish his career in a Heat uniform.

"I have thought about it, of course," Wade said when asked by the *Miami Herald* if he wanted to finish his career here either on the court or with a one-day contract. "I wouldn't lie and say I haven't. When that opportunity comes, that day comes, hopefully, I can go out in a Miami Heat jersey. I

After a season in Chicago and half a season in Cleveland, Dwyane Wade rejoined the Miami Heat in February 2018, much to the delight of Heat fans at AmericanAirlines Arena.

don't know how it will be, but I would love it."

Wade said last week that "this team plays hard. They're consistent with their game for the most part. That's going to get them a lot of wins. I'm impressed with the guys, J-Rich [Josh Richardson] and taking that step to the next level. Tyler [Johnson], playing amazing. I'm happy for those guys. But I expect it. I expect those guys to play the way they are."

On coach Erik Spoelstra, Wade said: "He never gets the credit. I'm not saying he's looking for it. He didn't get credit when we were winning championships and going to Finals. It's not easy to have success in this league. Last year, everyone thought he should have been Coach of the Year for what he was able to do. For what they're doing this year, he's right back up there in that conversation. He's a great coach. He's one of the best in our game. Those players who play their whole career there one day will be happy to know they were coached by a great coach."

The Heat drafted Wade with the fifth overall pick in the 2003 NBA Draft, and he spent his first 13 seasons with the team, winning three NBA championships with the Heat before playing the 2016–17 season with Chicago and the first part of this season with Cleveland.

Earlier in the day, the Heat traded injured forward Okaro White to Atlanta for Luke Babbitt, whose 44 percent three-point shooting ranks fifth among all NBA players who have made at least 40 three-pointers. Miami was 31–24 with Babbitt as a starter last season. ■

Wade shoots around during practice after returning to the Miami Heat in early 2018, as fans and photographers flock to capture his warmup.

Back in It in a Flash

Heat Rides Dwyane Wade to Game 2 Victory in Philly

By Manny Navarro · April 16, 2018

PHILADELPHIA—Dwyane Wade is 36—and he's still got some playoff magic in his bag.

Bound for Basketball's Hall of Fame in the not-so-distant future, the Heat's hero of heroes delivered another amazing playoff performance to lift Miami to a breathtaking 113–103 victory over the Philadephia 76ers in Game 2 of their first-round series Monday night at Wells Fargo Center.

Wade scored 28 points on 11 of 17 shooting and had seven rebounds, three assists and two steals in 26 minutes off the bench. And the Heat needed every ounce of it to hold off Ben Simmons and the talented young Sixers.

"He's different when you put him in a Miami Heat uniform," Heat coach Erik Spoelstra said. "I don't care what his numbers were anywhere else or all year long or at different times. He's for these moments."

Wade had a lot of special moments Monday night.

He started it by making his first seven shots.

Then, after scoring 21 points to rally the Heat from a nine-point deficit to a 56–42 halftime lead, Wade took the game over again in the fourth quarter after Philadelphia, winners of 17 in a row coming in, had trimmed the Heat's 16-point lead to 98–96 on an Ersan Ilyasova tip-in with 4:29 remaining.

In a flash, Wade stripped the ball from Dario Saric and scored on a dunk, found a wide-open James Johnson for another slam moments later and then grabbed an offensive rebound before Goran Dragić hit a jumpshot. Suddenly, the Heat's lead was 104–96.

"I think Dwyane's steal changed the game," Sixers coach Brett Brown said. "If you had to pick one defining moment, one defining play, I think it was that."

Moments later, Wade put the game on ice with a fadeaway 23-foot jumper with 47.9 seconds to play.

"I just came in with an aggressive approach," Wade said. "Whatever minutes I was going to play I was going to be aggressive. As [Justise] Winslow told me the other night, 'Empty the clip.' I emptied it."

Coming home with a split on the road was big for the Heat. Miami is 10–6 all time when a seven-game series starts 1–1 and 1–4 when it falls behind 0–2 (the only series win came in the 2006 NBA Finals vs. the Mavericks).

After being back with the Miami Heat for only two months, Dwyane Wade, the 36-year-old, three-time NBA champion recaptured some of his old playoff magic in Game 2 of the first round of the playoffs against the Philadelphia 76ers.

Game 3 is Thursday in Miami.

The Heat had a lot it wanted to improve upon after getting crushed by the Sixers in Game 1.

It started with defense and keeping the Sixers off the three-point line.

Philadelphia, which made 18 of its 28 three-point attempts in Game 1, finished 7 of 36 from beyond the arc and shot 41.7 percent overall in Game 2. After collecting 35 assists on Saturday and scoring 130 points (the most the Heat has ever allowed), Philly finished with 22 assists Monday.

"They responded as we talked about, as I anticipated," Brown said. "I give the Miami Heat credit in relation to the physicality of that game. I think their ball pressure and standing up our passes was excellent. I think Dwyane Wade offensively was just vintage Dwyane Wade."

Wade wasn't the only Heat player to provide some scoring punch Monday night. Six players finished in double figures for the Heat.

Dragić, who was 4 of 14 shooting for 15 points in Game 1, had a more efficient night with 20 points on 8 of 14 shooting.

Richardson, held to four points on 1 of 7 shooting Saturday, bounced back with 14 points, including eight in the third quarter as the Heat took an 86–75 lead into the fourth quarter.

Johnson followed up his 13-point Game 1 performance with 18 points (7 of 7 shooting), seven rebounds and five assists on Monday.

Center Hassan Whiteside, who had only two points, six rebounds, and played only 12 minutes in Game 1, finished with four points, five rebounds and one block in 15 minutes Monday. He picked

up his fourth foul with 9:25 left to play in the third quarter and watched from the bench the rest of the game. But Spoelstra liked Whiteside's minutes.

"His activity level was superb," he said. "Without those 15 minutes it might have been totally different. Those were much needed. He got that fourth foul, and I had the intention to put him back in the fourth. We just didn't get around to it when they made their run. They went even smaller. But we can definitely build on that."

Simmons finished with 24 points to lead the Sixers. Saric had 23.

Just like they did in the second half of Saturday night's blowout of the Heat, Philadelphia opened the game with Ilyasova at center and immediately began attacking the rim as Whiteside and his teammates went out on the perimeter to try and stop another Philly three-point barrage.

The Sixers' offense took advantage of Whiteside's presence away from the paint early.

As the Heat racked up fouls (the first eight fouls of the game were called on Miami), the Sixers built a 29–22 lead off 18 points in the paint and 12 second-chance points off six offensive rebounds. But things quickly changed in the second quarter.

The Heat began applying full-court pressure with Winslow leading the charge, and the Heat didn't allow the Sixers much room to operate at all on the three-point line.

Miami outscored Philadelphia 34–13 in the second quarter and held the Sixers to 4 of 21 shooting in the period and 2 of 18 shooting from three-point range for the half.

All the while, Wade couldn't miss. He led an

18–2 Heat run to open the second quarter and had 21 points on 8 of 9 shooting at the break in only 12 minutes and 24 seconds of work.

Said Whiteside: "I've been saying it for a while now, 'It's good to be back in the playoffs with my brother.' There's no purple-shirt guy this time." ■

Wade scored 28 points on 11 of 17 shooting, had seven rebounds, three assists and two steals in 26 minutes off the bench in the Heat's 113–103 Game 2 first-round playoff victory over the 76ers.

Dwyane Wade Reminds Us Why We'll Miss Him

His Team-High 21 Not Enough in Heartbreaking Home Opener for Miami Heat

By Greg Cote · October 20, 2018

Dwyane Wade is calling this "the last dance"—his final Heat season playing before Miami fans.

It began Saturday. The dance was not a waltz. It was exhausting. It was exhilarating. It was all of that, in waves.

It was a crushing and bad loss in Miami's 31st home opener, 113–112 to Charlotte, but also one noble in its improbable Heat comeback from a 26-point third-quarter hole.

Mostly, it was D-Wade, reminding us why we'll miss him.

It was Wade, off the bench with a team-high 21 points on 9 for 15 shooting, including his first two three-point shots of the season in the closing minutes.

This was just the start, suggesting it's going to be a wild ride, indeed.

The Heat finds itself living in the Curse of Pretty Good right now, or of trying to get there. Seemingly about a thousand miles from the next championship parade down Biscayne Boulevard.

The immediate upside that fans are left to hope their team can creep up into the mid-40s on season victories and maybe win a playoff series.

Optimism for that and something less both presented themselves in Saturday's home opener, a dispiriting loss to a Hornets team Miami thought itself better than only to be schooled otherwise. The sold-out home crowd came looking for a party of a start to Wade's farewell season only to depart far too quietly into the night, left to wonder what has happened to the team that sat atop the sport in the king's chair in 2011–14.

The is life in the modern NBA when one superteam at a time reigns, and it's Golden State's time and that's it. No complaints from South Florida, please. Miami invented the template with the Big 3, and now is left to navigate forward with something closer to the Big *Nada*. Miami is today a starless team in a star-dependent league, apart from the used-to-be-glow of the 36-year-old Wade, who now comes in off the bench.

As if to verify that Miami is trying to win with a

In his final home opener with the Miami Heat and in his career, Dwyane Wade shot 9 of 15 from the floor for a team-high 21 points in the Heat's heartbreaking 113–112 loss to the Charlotte Hornets.

patchwork of effort, coaching, depth, and "culture," the Heat's early-season starting lineup features zero first-round draft picks.

Most teams pretty good or better have a reliable go-to presence. Charlotte has Kemba Walker.

Miami hopes somebody will shine each night, never quite sure who that reliably might be. The Heat's late, failed effort to trade for available Jimmy Butler further reminded that Pat Riley from his high perch sees exactly what his team is missing.

Wade drives past an off-balance Charlotte Hornets defender in Miami's 2018–2019 home opener at AmericanAirlines Arena.

Wade, even at his age, was almost it Saturday. *Almost.*

The Heat at 1–2 with 79 games to play, the team in the Curse of Pretty Good or trying to get there, presents a particular challenge for Miami fans who'd grown accustomed to national relevance.

It isn't all bad. It forces one to not fast-forward to the assumed eventuality—NBA Finals or bust!—but to instead enjoy the mystery and the hidden corners on the long ride to whatever fate holds.

Reasons to watch along the way:

1. Wade and Udonis Haslem's long good-bye, of which Saturday night was quite literally the beginning of the end. Wade entered the game mid-first quarter to a standing ovation. Later there was a vintage minute when he scored on a reverse layup that left him sprawled on his back, and then on a fall-away baseline jumper. He finished strong to mint his best game of the newborn season.

"Heat Nation, what up?" Wade spoke to the adoring crowd before the game, Haslem at his side. "My brother and I want to thank each and every one of you guys. It's meant so much to us."

Vintage Wade or less, winning season or not, the epic heft of Wade and Haslem's final home game will grow as it nears by degrees, the emotional pull of the season.

2. The Heat, of the franchise pedigree, even fighting the Curse of Pretty Good, might still be the surest bet to make the playoffs of any major South Florida team. Would you bet the Dolphins, Panthers, Marlins, or Heat right now? *Exactly.* As they showed in fighting back from a 26-point hole Saturday, this team *will* compete.

3. Can Josh Richardson grow into stardom? He seemed cast for the role the first two games, seemingly anointed by Wade.

"They're telling me to be aggressive," Richardson says.

Haslem on J-Rich: "He's stepping up on offense and still taking the challenge defensively. Guys do not do that in this league anymore."

Saturday, the (apparent) chosen one was quiet with seven points.

4. Will young Bam Adebayo and Justise Winslow blossom? Along with Richardson, these are the two who must become stars if the Heat is to grow to win big with the present nucleus. Adebayo is the man who must make Hassan Whiteside expendable when his contract expires after next season. The team just reinvested in Winslow, extending his rookie contract by three years.

5. Full health, please. And will Dion Waiters ever play again?

Where it ends, nobody knows.
The surest bet?
Through the tears of farewell or the memories he's yet to create, Dwyane Wade will be the Heat's star. *Again.* ■

One Last Team-Up

LeBron and D-Wade Will Team Up One Final Time at All-Star Game

By Anthony Chiang and David Wilson · February 7, 2019

Sacramento—Dwyane Wade and LeBron James will share the court one final time February 17 and, for the first time since the Big 3 broke up in 2014, it will be as teammates.

For the second straight year, the NBA held a draft to determine the rosters for the All-Star Game and this year the league used the third round of the draft to let the captains pick from "special roster additions" Wade and Dallas Mavericks forward Dirk Nowitzki. With the first pick in the final round, James chose to reunite two-thirds of the Miami Heat's Big 3.

"Everyone in the world knows who I'm going with. I'm going with Dirk," James said during the prerecorded draft before bursting out into laughter. "I'm just kidding. I'm going with my buddy Dwyane Wade."

After Thursday's practice in Sacramento, Wade said, "It's only right" he's on Team LeBron.

"I'm going to enjoy it," Wade said. "My only goal All-Star Weekend is to try to throw LeBron one lob because that's what everybody wants to see. Outside of that, I don't need to do much else, maybe guard Dirk once."

James and Wade, of course, played together in Miami from 2010 to 2014, helping the Heat, along with forward Chris Bosh, win two NBA titles in four seasons.

The two's friendship traces back further than just when they finally united in South Florida. James was the No. 1 overall selection by the Cleveland Cavaliers in the 2003 NBA Draft, and Miami took Wade with the No. 5 pick in the same draft. In 2004, they played for the bronze medal–winning United States Olympic team, then reunited again in 2008 to win gold in Athens. Two years later, Wade convinced James and Bosh to come play with him.

They were All-Star teammates for all four of those seasons, plus the five before and two after when James was with the Cavaliers. Wade, however, missed the game the last two seasons while James was wrapping up his second stint in Cleveland. In his final season in the NBA, Wade will get to play in his final All-Star Game, though, thanks to commissioner Adam Silver's special invitation Friday for the three-time champion guard and Nowitzki, a former champion in his own right. Once it became clear James would have the opportunity to take Wade, there was never really much of a doubt what would happen.

Dwyane Wade and LeBron James look on during the trophy presentation ceremony after Team LeBron's 178–164 win over Team Giannis during the 2019 NBA All-Star Game on February 17 in Charlotte, North Carolina.

"He better pick me," Wade said Friday after the Heat's loss to the Oklahoma City Thunder at AmericanAirlines Arena. "I'm not even going to play. He better pick me. I'm not going to play this game."

This season, Wade is averaging 14.0 points per game in a reserve role for Miami. He could, however, be an option to start for the Heat (25–27) moving forward after Miami dealt guards Tyler Johnson and Wayne Ellington to the Phoenix Suns on Wednesday.

The starters for Wade's team, which was drafted by James: Golden State Warriors forward Kevin Durant, Boston Celtics guard Kyrie Irving, Toronto Raptors wing Kawhi Leonard, Houston Rockets guard James Harden and James. Milwaukee Bucks forward Giannis Antetokounmpo, the other captain, picked Warriors guard Stephen Curry, Philadelphia 76ers post player Joel Embiid, Oklahoma City Thunder swingman Paul George and Charlotte Hornets point guard Kemba Walker as his other starters.

Team LeBron also includes New Orleans Pelicans post player Anthony Davis, Golden State wing Klay Thompson, 76ers point Ben Simmons, Portland Trail Blazers point guard Damian Lillard, San Antonio Spurs post player LaMarcus Aldridge, Minnesota Timberwolves center Karl-Antony Towns and Washington Wizards shooting guard Bradley Beal.

Team Giannis also includes Bucks wing Khris Middleton, Denver Nuggets post player Nikola Jokic, Thunder point guard Russell Westbrook, Brooklyn Nets guard D'Angelo Russell, Orlando Magic post player Nikola Vucevic and Raptors point guard Kyle Lowry.

Antetokounmpo originally drafted Simmons before James proposed swapping him for Westbrook. Eventually, they came to an agreement, but not before Antetokounmpo played some hardball.

His pitch: "What if you put Dwyane Wade in the trade?" ■

Wade points to a teammate during the second quarter of the 2019 NBA All-Star Game, Wade's 13th and final All-Star Game.